D0708640

2009/1

pay
less
tax

Paul Lewis

To my father
who encouraged my love of numbers

Contents

Published in 2009 by Age Concern Books

1268 London Road, London, SW16 4ER, United Kingdom

ISBN: 978 0 86242 446-6

A catalogue record for this book is available from the British Library.

While every effort has been made to ensure that all the information contained in this book is true and accurate at the time of going to press, neither Age Concern England nor the author can accept any legal responsibility or liability for any errors or omissions, or changes to any procedure or law that occur after publication. Reference to any agencies, products or services in this book does not constitute a recommendation by Age Concern.

Edited by Marie Shields

Cover design by Vincent McEvoy

Designed and typeset by Design and Media Solutions, Maidstone

Printed and bound in Great Britain by Bell & Bain Ltd, Glasgow

The four national Age Concerns in the UK have joined together with Help the Aged to form new national charities dedicated to improving the lives of older people.

Mixed Sources
Product group from well-managed forests and other controlled sources
www.fsc.org   Cert no. TT-COC-002769
© 1996 Forest Stewardship Council

FSC

Author

Paul Lewis is a freelance financial journalist who writes and broadcasts widely on personal finance issues. He presents *Money Box* on Radio 4 and writes regularly for *Saga Magazine* and its website.

He writes for the BBC website and appears regularly on BBC One's breakfast programme and various radio stations. He speaks widely at meetings of the financial services industry. His other books include *Money Magic* and *Live Long and Prosper*. He also writes *Beat the Banks*, published by Age Concern.

Introduction

Who wrote it?

I have been writing and broadcasting about personal finance for more than 25 years, and I have one job – to help readers and listeners keep more of their own money. Over the years, I have saved thousands of people hundreds of thousands of pounds by clear, honest advice about how personal finance – your money – works.

Why read it?

It will save you money. Every year people pay hundreds of millions of pounds too much tax. I love tax and the complexities of it all. I actually look forward to Budget Day. This book will help you pay less. Not by cheating or lying or hiding things. But just by making sure that you pay the right amount at the right time. If you have paid too much tax, it explains how to claim it back. After all, it's your money.

Who pays tax?

Most people. If you're under 65, you normally pay tax on any income over £124 a week. If you're 65 or more, anything over £182 a week is taxed. Even if your income is less than that, tax is automatically taken off some things. Your bank or building society deducts 20% off the interest on your savings, and money you earn or get from a pension can have tax deducted before you see it. These automatic deductions are often wrong – that can mean you pay too much tax.

Isn't it all horribly complicated?

With a bit of time and the occasional help of a calculator, I honestly believe anyone can understand tax.

Look at it this way. There's a tenner lying on the floor. Do you go to the effort of bending down and picking it up? Or just say 'Can't be bothered' and leave it there. The effort it takes to read this book is like bending down to pick up a tenner.

Deep down, tax is simple. But politicians, lawyers and accountants spend their working lives making it more complicated. That's their job and it helps all of them take money off us; sometimes when they shouldn't. This book will help you get back money you should never have paid in the first place.

What does it cover?

This book is about five major taxes that drain our bank accounts and which we can reduce:

Income Tax – nearly half of people aged 60 or more pay Income Tax. It is due on your income from pensions (including the State Pension), earnings, interest on savings, some social security benefits, and rent you are paid by tenants and some lodgers. This book explains tax allowances and the rates of tax, and shows you how to work out how much tax you should pay – and how to claim it back if you have paid too much. It explains tax codes and tax for people who are self-employed (pages 77–87). It also, of course, explains self-assessment, which can apply to people who are self-employed, have untaxed income from savings, pay tax at the higher rate of 40%, or in some cases just have an income above £22,900. In a growing number of cases, some people who just get the State Pension are sent a self-assessment form.

National Insurance contributions (pages 53–57) – these must be paid by men under 65 and women under 60 if they work and earn more than £110 a week, or if they are self-employed and earn more than £97 a week.

Capital Gains Tax (CGT) (pages 88–94) – very few people pay CGT each year, but it can sneak up on you. It is a tax on the growth in value of something you own and is normally due when you get rid of it – either by selling it or giving it away. It can also apply if you get a sudden windfall from a mutual insurance business when it converts from a society to a company.

Inheritance Tax (IHT – pages 95–106) – is charged on the money and property you leave when you die. Few estates are liable to IHT but, like CGT, it can take people with fairly modest means by surprise, and the increase in house prices in recent years means that more people fear being caught by it. This book explains how to reduce the risk of your relatives losing out when you die, and the rules which make it less of a burden to married couples.

Stamp Duty Land Tax (SDLT) (pages 107–109) – often just called stamp duty, SDLT is normally charged on any home that is bought for more than £125,000. But until 2 September 2009 the limit is raised to £175,000. There are a few ways to reduce it.

These five taxes are collected by Her Majesty's Revenue & Customs (HMRC), which I call just 'the Revenue' in this book. Pages 110–116 give information about contacting the Revenue and what to do when things go wrong – as they often do.

The book does not cover taxes on things we buy, such as Value Added Tax (VAT); the duties on alcohol, tobacco and petrol; airport passenger duty charged on air tickets; or insurance premium tax paid on some premiums for some kinds of insurance. Nor does it cover stamp duty on shares or the annual road tax we pay for every vehicle we own. There is not much you can do about those taxes – except give up the things that are taxed.

It's not about council tax (or rates in Northern Ireland). That is set and collected by your local council and there are ways you can reduce the amount you pay. To find out how, contact the Age Concern Information Line on 0800 00 99 66 (8am–7pm, seven days a week).

Is it up to date?

No book on tax can guarantee that the rules haven't changed since it was written. But the information should be accurate for the tax year 6 April 2009 to 5 April 2010. It incorporates the changes announced in the 2009 Budget.

If you are completing a tax return for 2008/09 – which will normally have arrived in April 2009 – you will need to know last tax year's rates and allowances too. They are at the end (pages 117–119).

If you live abroad – or pretend you do to avoid tax – this book is not for you. The information in this guide only applies to people who live in the UK and are what the Revenue calls 'domiciled' here. That means the UK is where your roots – and your heart – are.

Paul Lewis

Income Tax

Your income is assessed for tax over the 'tax year' which runs from 6 April to the following 5 April. If you want to know why that year is used, it dates back to the reform of the calendar in 1752 when 11 days were taken out of September to get the calendar back in line with the seasons. The year started then on 25 March and so did the tax year. But when 11 days were removed, the tax year had to be the same length so the start was pushed forward 11 days from 25 March to 6 April. At the same time the calendar year was moved to start on 1 January.

This book covers the rules that apply for the tax year 6 April 2009 to 5 April 2010 – usually written '2009/10'.

The principle behind Income Tax is simple. You are allowed a certain amount of income each year without paying tax on it at all. The rest of your income is taxed; and the bigger your income, the higher the rate of tax you pay on it. The detailed way in which the system works is very complicated, though, and often leaves experts scratching their heads. This section explains the rules and shows you how to work out whether you should pay any tax at all, and if so how much. It also explains how to claim tax back if you have paid more than you should have done.

Which income is tax free?

Some types of income have no tax due on them.
However much you have of that sort of income,
you needn't worry about tax. The Revenue calls it
'non-taxable' income and it includes:

- **Social security benefits that depend on your
  income** – they are Council Tax Benefit, Housing
  Benefit, Pension Credit (over age 60), Income
  Support (under age 60), and income-related
  Employment and Support Allowance.

Money-saving tip: *More than three million
people aged over 60 do not claim the help
they could get with their Council Tax, their
rent or their income in general. Up to £5
billion goes unclaimed each year. Ask for
advice at your local Age Concern or
Citizens Advice Bureau, call the Pension
Credit line on 0800 99 1234 or look online
at www.entitledto.com, which will help you
work out what you can claim.*

- **Child Tax Credit (for people with children)
  and Working Tax Credit (for people in
  low-paid work)** have special rules to help those
  aged over 50 who return to work.
  Tax credits are paid by the Revenue but
  have nothing to do with tax. They depend on
  your household income and are paid directly to
  the householder or the main carer of the child.

Money-saving tip: *Tax credits are hard
to understand and work out. If you have a
dependent child or low pay, you may be*

able to claim. Call the Tax Credits Helpline on 0845 300 3900 (0845 603 2000 in Northern Ireland) or look online at www.entitledto.com, *which will help you work out what you can claim.*

- **Most benefits paid because of a disability or illness** – these include Attendance Allowance, Disability Living Allowance (care and mobility components), Industrial Injuries Scheme Benefits, War Disablement Pension, War Widow's Pension, Severe Disablement Allowance, Independent Living Fund payments and other disablement pensions from the police, fire brigade and merchant navy. Incapacity Benefit is tax free if you claimed it before 13 April 1995 and have claimed it continuously since. Income-related Employment and Support Allowance is tax free.

Money-saving tip: *Lots of people could claim disability benefits but do not do so. When you claim, be honest about what you can and cannot do. Many people downplay their problems and that can stop them getting the benefits they are entitled to. Your local Age Concern or Citizens Advice Bureau can help you claim.*

- **The £10 Christmas Bonus** paid in December with the State Pension and some other benefits and the extra £60 paid early in 2009.
- **The Winter Fuel Payment** for people aged 60 or older.

Money-saving tip: *You can get the £200 Winter Fuel Payment for winter 2009 if your date of birth is 27 September 1949 or earlier. If you qualify for the first time this year, the Department for Work and Pensions may not know about you. Call 08459 15 15 15 to let them know – have your National Insurance number handy. Look online at* www.thepensionservice.gov.uk/winterfuel *to find out more.*

- **The £2,000 Bereavement Payment** which a husband or wife may get when their partner dies.
- **Child Benefit.**
- **Some investment income** – including the gains on National Savings certificates and interest on an Individual Savings Account (ISA) (see pages 33–34).
- **If you rent out a room in your home**, up to £4,250 of rent in the year is normally tax free. The person you rent to must share your home, perhaps sharing the kitchen or bathroom and some living space, and must not be a tenant. You need not declare the income if it is no more than £4,250 (though if you get a self-assessment form you may have to enter it there) but you cannot claim any expenses in connection with the let. Look online at *www.direct.gov.uk* and put 'rent a room' in the search box.
- **Prizes from gambling** – including winnings on Premium Bonds, football pools, racing and the

National Lottery. But if you make your living from gambling, the income can be taxable.

Money-saving tip: *Don't gamble. The odds are always in favour of the bookie or casino and new higher rates of tax on gambling companies from April 2007 mean there is less money left for them to pay out in winnings.*

- **Gifts** – even gifts of money you receive regularly. But if you are given money in exchange for doing work or providing a service, then that is counted as earnings and is taxable. In rare circumstances, a gift of money may be liable to Inheritance Tax.
- **Maintenance payments** made to a divorced or separated spouse or civil partner, or to children.
- **If you are made redundant**, the first £30,000 of any redundancy payment is tax free and the rest is taxable. But if you are entitled to a leaving payment under your contract of employment, then the whole of it will be taxed before you receive it. The Revenue may challenge the exemption on redundancy money if it considers that your redundancy was not genuine: for example, if it was in fact early retirement.

Tax-saving tip: *If the Revenue questions the tax-free status of a redundancy payment, challenge it. Get advice, as the Revenue does make mistakes.*

5

- **A lump sum** for an injury or disability that prevents you from continuing to work.

- **A payment made when you leave a job** where you mainly worked abroad.

- **Dividends paid on shares** are taxed in a strange way. Tax is already taken off the dividend before you get it and there is no tax to pay for people who pay basic rate tax or below. Higher-rate taxpayers will have to pay extra tax on dividends (see pages 32 and 119).

Which income is normally taxed?

All other income may be taxed if you have more than a certain amount of it. The Revenue calls it 'taxable income' and it includes:

- **Wages, salary and any other bonuses** or payments given to you for work you have done.

- **The profit you make** as a self-employed person.

- **The State Pension.**

- **Any pension from your job**, any personal pension or any other pension which you have paid into.

- **Social security benefits that replace pay** – these include Bereavement Allowance, Carer's Allowance, Statutory Sick Pay, Maternity Pay and maternity benefits, and Employment and Support Allowance in some cases.

- **The interest on savings and investments** – including any investments held abroad, apart from the exceptions listed above in the non-taxable section.
- **The rent you receive from property you own** – except for the rent-a-room scheme (see page 4). If you do not come under the rent-a-room scheme, then you can deduct any expenses before the income is taxed.

What are tax allowances?

Each year we are allowed to have a certain amount of taxable income before any tax is due. These amounts are also called 'personal allowances' and every individual – men and women, married or single, living with someone or alone, aged 2 or 92 – gets one. Although they are called 'allowances', they are not an amount of money you are given – they are the amount of taxable income you are allowed to have before you have to start paying tax on it.

In 2009/10 the personal allowances are:

Tax allowances 2009/10	
Age 0 to 64	£6,475
Age 65 to 74 on 5/4/2009	£9,490
Age 75 or more on 5/4/2009	£9,640
Blind person – add	£1,890

So if you are aged 65 and your total income from earnings, pensions and interest amounts to

£9,490 or less, then you should not have to pay Income Tax. If it amounts to more than that, then Income Tax will be due on the excess. This allowance for people over 65 has increased by more than £400 in 2009/10. So even if you have paid tax before, you may no longer have to do so.

Income above your personal allowance is taxed at one of five rates, depending on:

- how much there is; and
- where it comes from.

Rates of Income Tax 2008/09	
Income on top of allowance	**Rate of tax**
Up to £37,400 – basic rate	20% on all income. However, dividends are taxed at 10%. And if you have interest on savings and your other income is not more than £2,440 above your tax allowance then up to £2,440 of the interest can be taxed at 10%, the rest at 20%.
Above £37,400 – higher rate	40% on all income (except dividends which are taxed at 32.5%)

Everything in tax has little quirks. So let's look at the allowances in a bit more detail.

People aged 65 and over

You can claim the higher personal allowance for a whole tax year (6 April to 5 April) if you reach 65 or 75 at any time during the year and your income is below a certain level (see below).

So if you were born before 6 April 1945, you can claim the higher allowance in 2009/10. If you were born before 6 April 1935, you can claim the higher allowance for people over 75.

Tax-saving tip: *The Revenue should know your date of birth, but it does not always get it right. So if you will be 65 or 75 between 6 April 2009 and 5 April 2010, check that you get the right tax allowance this tax year. Normally the Revenue will not give you the allowance in the year you become eligible. It will give it to you the following year and sort out the overpayment then. So make sure you ask for it this year – if you ask, you will get it.*

But – and it is a big but – one of the most annoying things about this higher allowance is that you lose it if your income is above a certain level:

- The personal allowance will be reduced if what is called your 'total gross income' is more than £22,900. We explain how to work that out later.

- For every £2 of extra income above £22,900 your allowance will be reduced by £1. For example, if you are 65 and your total income is £1,000 above the limit, then your allowance will be reduced by £1,000 ÷ 2 = £500. So it will be £9,490 - £500 = £8,990.

£ It will be reduced to £6,475 if your income is £28,930 or more (aged 65 to 74) or £29,230 or more (aged 75 or over).

£ The allowance is never reduced below the basic personal allowance of £6,475.

If your personal allowance is reduced because your income is over £22,900, you can end up paying tax at a very high rate. Income between £22,900 and £28,930 (£29,230 over 75) is in fact taxed at 30%. It works like this:

£ Each additional £2 of income is taxed at 20% and it also reduces your tax allowance by £1, bringing another £1 of income liable to tax. The result is that each £2 increase in income above £22,900 results in tax on £3 of income. At 20% that is 60p. So for each £2 of income, your tax rises by 60p or 30% on that £2.

Tax-saving tip: *If you are married, consider moving assets between you to make sure that neither spouse has an income above £22,900. The £22,900 income limit applies separately to the income of each member of a couple (see the example of Sid and Lillian on pages 72–76).*

Total gross income

If you are a basic rate taxpayer aged 65 or over and you want to see if you are entitled to the higher tax allowances for your age group, you cannot just add up the income you receive. As explained earlier, you have to work out what is called 'total gross income'.

To do that, any savings income which has had tax already deducted must have that tax added back. That process is called 'grossing up'. Every £80 of net interest you receive is treated by the tax office as £100 gross income because £20 tax has been taken off it. **So to 'gross up' your net savings income, divide by 4 and multiply by 5.**

Matthew *is 65 and retired from work in March 2009. His income for the year from state and occupational pensions totals £8,990. As he is 65, his tax allowance is £9,490. He also gets interest from a bank account, which he expects to be £464 this year. So he thinks his total income is £9,454, which is just below his tax allowance, and he expects to pay no tax. But he has forgotten to gross up his additional income from interest. If he divides it by 4 and multiplies by 5, he gets £580, which takes his total income up to £9,570. Tax will be deducted from all his savings income. But he will be able to claim a repayment of most of it (see pages 28–30 for more details).*

If you get dividends on shares, then you must also use the gross dividend to work out if you are entitled to the higher allowance.

On the other hand, you can deduct some income. You can take off any payments to charity made under Gift Aid. Because Gift Aid payments come out of your taxed income, you must work out the amount before tax and you do that by dividing by 4 and multiplying by 5.

ⓔ So if you paid £100 under Gift Aid, you divide by 4 and multiply by 5 which gives £125 and you can deduct that from your income (there is more on Gift Aid on page 19).

You can also deduct any payments you make yourself into a pension scheme. Again, work out the amount before tax. Remember you can pay into a pension up to age 75 regardless of whether you are retired or not.

After grossing up your interest and deducting gift aid and pension contributions, you get your total gross income, which is used to assess whether you are entitled to a higher allowance and how much it will be. Some tax offices have been getting the rules about deducting Gift Aid payments wrong. Make sure yours gets it right.

Blind Person's Allowance

A person registered as blind with their local authority gets an extra tax allowance of £1,890, but they must claim it from their tax office.

That means a blind person can have an extra £1,890 income in 2009/10 before starting to pay tax.

ⓔ So someone aged 74 who is blind can have an income of £9,490 + £1,890 = £11,380 before any tax is due.

A married blind person whose income is too low to use up the tax allowance can transfer it to their spouse or civil partner. If both partners are blind, they can each get the £1,890 and either one can transfer it to the other if they cannot use it in full.

Tax-saving tip: *If you or your spouse is blind, make sure you get the extra allowance.*

You may be able to register as blind with your local council even when you are not totally without sight. To be registered, you must show that your lack of sight makes it impossible to perform any work for which eyesight is essential. The Revenue can also give you the allowance if you have applied to be registered as blind but this has not yet been granted. You do not, though, get the Blind Person's Allowance if you are registered with your local council as partially sighted. The rules and procedures about registration are different in England, Wales, Scotland and Northern Ireland, so contact your local council for more details.

Married Couple's Allowance

The Married Couple's Allowance was abolished in April 2000 for most married couples. But some older couples can still get it if either partner was born before 6 April 1935; so one partner has to 75 at some point in the tax year. To qualify for the Married Couple's Allowance the couple must live together and, of course, be married or civil partners.

Since 5 December 2005, two men or two women can form a 'civil partnership' which essentially gives them all the rights and responsibilities of marriage. It is not called marriage and they are not called spouses (or husbands or wives come to that). However, whenever this book refers to marriage or spouses, it includes civil partnerships and civil partners, most of whom think of themselves as married spouses anyway.

Despite its name, the Married Couple's Allowance is not like the personal allowance. It is simply a deduction off the tax that is due. It is now set at one level. Before 2009/10 there was a lower rate for those aged under 75 in the tax year. But in 2009/10 anyone old enough to qualify must be at least 75 at some point in the tax year. So the lower rate is no longer paid.

Married Couple's Allowance 2009/10		
Age of older partner on 5/4/10	**Allowance**	**Tax deduction**
75 or more	£6,965	£696.50
Minimum amount	£2,670	£267.00

The deduction is made after the tax due for the year is worked out.

The Married Couple's Allowance is available to those who marry or form a civil partnership now, as long as at least one of the partners was born before 6 April 1935. If the marriage takes place before 6 May, the full allowance is available in the tax year they marry. If they marry on or after 6 May, the allowance is reduced by one-twelfth for each whole 'tax month' starting on the 6th of each month. In subsequent years they get the full allowance.

Which partner gets the Married Couple's Allowance depends on when they were married.

- **For married couples who qualified before 5 December 2005**, the Married Couple's Allowance is given to the husband. But a married woman can choose to have up to £1,335 of it herself if she asks (worth £133.50 off her tax) and can have £2,670 (worth £267 off her tax) with her husband's consent (it may be the 21st century but these are 20th century rules!). The rest has to be taken off the husband's tax.

- **For couples (married or civil partners) who first qualified for the Married Couple's Allowance on 5 December 2005 or later**, it is given to the partner with the higher income. The other partner can choose to have up to £1,335 of it if they ask (worth £133.50 off their tax) and can have £2,670 (worth £267 off their tax) with the other partner's consent. The balance has to be taken off the entitled partner's tax. Any change in the allocation of the Married Couple's Allowance under this rule must be done before the start of the tax year, so it is too late now for 2009/10, but you could do it for 2010/11. Once you have made the choice it will continue to operate in the same way until you make a different choice.

 Get Revenue Form 18, *Transferring the Married Couple's Tax Allowance.*

Under a separate rule, a partner who gets the Married Couple's Allowance can transfer some or all of it to the other partner if their own income is too low to make use of it. That might be useful if a wife has a higher income than her husband does and he pays very little tax or none at all.

This transfer is made using form 575, Notice of transfer of surplus Income Tax allowances (which you can get online at www.hmrc.gov.uk/forms/575-t-man.pdf). It can be done up to six years afterwards, so in 2009/10 you can look back to 2003/04 to adjust the allocation of the Married Couple's Allowance.

Gerard *is 76 and his wife* **Clara** *is 71. Gerard has a State Pension of £102.30 a week and a pension from his job of £215.25 a month. They have no savings. His total annual income is £7,902.60. He is over 75 and his income is well below his personal allowance of £9,640. So he has no tax to pay and cannot use the Married Couple's Allowance deduction.*

Clara has her own State Pension of £94.70 a week and a pension from her job in the civil service of £642.30 a month. So her annual income is £12,632. As she is 71, she gets a personal allowance of £9,490 and pays tax of £628.40 this year.

But if they ask to transfer the Married Couple's Allowance to Clara, she gets the full £696.50 deducted off her tax, so she pays none at all (saving her more than £52 a month). She asks for that to be done for earlier years too – right back to 2003/04 – and they get a cheque from the Revenue for more than £2,000.

The transfer is unlikely to be of use to people who first qualified from 5 December 2005, as the partner with the higher income will automatically be the one who is entitled to the Married Couple's Allowance.

But – just as with the higher personal allowances – the Married Couple's Allowance is reduced if the entitled partner's income exceeds a certain amount.

£ The calculation depends on how old each partner is, but normally it is reduced if the entitled partner's income exceeds £29,230.

If income exceeds £37,820, the Married Couple's Allowance is reduced to £2,670 and there it stays – it cannot be reduced further.

The allowance is only reduced as a result of the level of income of the entitled partner, even if the other partner gets some of the allowance. The rules about working out your total gross income are the same as for the personal allowances and are explained on page 7.

Widows and widowers

There are no particular tax concessions for widows. A woman or a man who becomes widowed can continue to receive any Married Couple's Allowance that is due for that tax year, as can a bereaved civil partner. They can also receive any unused part of the Married Couple's Allowance that their partner was entitled to in that year. The deceased person's executors should make sure it is transferred.

Divorce

The Married Couple's Allowance is only available to married couples who live together. If a couple permanently separates, the allowance continues for the rest of that tax year and then stops. Normally the divorce will come after that and the allowance will already have stopped. But if a couple divorces without separating first, then the allowance stops in the tax year after the divorce.

If you make maintenance payments, they come out of your taxed income. There are no tax concessions unless one of the former partners was born before 6 April 1935 and the payment is made under a court order, a legally binding agreement, or an order of the Child Support Agency. In these circumstances the person who makes the payment can get a deduction off their tax of 10% of the value of the payment, up to a maximum of £267.

If you receive a maintenance payment of any sort you do not have to pay tax on it.

Mortgage payments and home income plans

Interest payments on a mortgage do not qualify for tax relief.

But if you have a home income plan you took out before 9 March 1999, then the payment of interest on the first £30,000 of that mortgage is reduced by tax relief:

- £ For every £1 you pay, the Revenue chips in 30p.

This amount is already taken into account as part of the payment you make and does not affect your other tax calculations.

Pension contributions

If you leave a job after less than six months, you will get a refund of the contributions you have paid into your employer's pension scheme. You can claim the refund if you have been paying into the scheme for less than two years – though that is probably not a good thing to do. Tax at 20% (or 40% on amounts over £10,800) will be deducted from the refund before it is paid to you.

Payments to charity

When you give any money to a charity, you will usually be asked to make the donation under Gift Aid rules. These rules enable the charity to claim back the basic rate tax you have already paid on the gift.

That boosts what you pay to the charity by 25% – if you give £10, the Chancellor will add £2.50 to your gift, and in 2009/10 another 32p as well.

Gift Aid only works if you pay as much tax as the tax relief on your gift. If you do not pay tax, then you cannot pay through Gift Aid. If you do, the Revenue will try to recover the tax wrongly paid back to the charity, and the charity – or even the Revenue – may try to recover from you the full amount you promised.

Tax-saving tip: *If you pay higher-rate tax, keep a receipt for any money you pay to a charity – including a single gift, however small, or a regular subscription. You can reclaim the higher-rate tax, which equals 25% of the amount you gave, through your self-assessment tax return.*

How is income taxed?

Income Tax is assessed over the whole tax year and in some ways it would be easier to pay none all year and then a lump sum at the end. But the Revenue likes to get its hands on our money as soon as it can – preferably without asking us first – and it has devised several ways of doing just that.

Earnings and pensions

The most thorough of these automatic tax systems is called 'PAYE' or Pay As You Earn – though it also applies to pensions. A study done by the Revenue in 2006/07 for the National Audit Office estimated that each year the Revenue deducts £500 million more tax than it should through PAYE. A year later the National Audit Office revealed that one in six tax codes is wrong.

PAYE covers wages and salaries, as well as payment of pensions from a previous job or a personal pension or retirement annuity contract we have paid into.

If you are self-employed, your profits will be taxed through the self-assessment system, described on pages 43–53, but your pension or any earnings will normally still be taxed through PAYE.

PAYE uses a system called a 'tax code', which your employer or pension payer uses to work out how much tax to deduct from your weekly or monthly payment. Tax codes are explained in more detail on pages 35–43.

Under PAYE, your annual tax allowance is divided by 12 (or 52 if you are paid weekly) so that each month (or week) you get some income free of tax, and the rest is taxed.

£ So if your personal tax allowance was £6,475 and you had no other taxable income, your employer would not tax the first £539.58 you earned each month but then would tax the rest.

Tax-saving tip: *A tax code is simply an approximate way of collecting tax; it is not an accurate way of assessing what you should pay. So you may end up with too much tax deducted from your money. Always check the code when you receive it and check the amount of tax you have paid at the end of the year.*

When you leave work

When you retire from work, your income will usually fall. If that happens during the tax year, you may qualify for a tax rebate – that is because the tax code system assumes you are paid much the same all year. So if your income drops, you may have had too much tax deducted in the first part of the year.

If the State Pension is your only income when you retire, send your P45 form to your tax office, along with details of your age, the date you retired, and your estimated total income from the day you retire until the next 5 April. If any refund is due, it will normally come directly from the tax office.

If you get a pension from a former employer, any tax rebate to which you are entitled for the tax year in which you retired will normally be paid by reducing the tax due on your occupational pension. If your pension provider does not receive enough information to do this by the end of the tax year in which you retired, any rebate will normally come direct from the tax office. Don't expect it to come automatically – write to the tax office if you think a repayment is due.

Tax-saving tip: *If your income falls significantly during the tax year make sure that the tax office knows as soon as possible.*

Retirement annuity contracts

If you started paying into a pension before 1 July 1988, it may be a retirement annuity contract (sometimes called a section 226 pension). They were personal pensions before that term was invented and you could have paid into one independently of your job or, if your employer did not have its own occupational pension, through your work. It may have been linked to a life insurance policy.

Until April 2007, these retirement annuity contract pensions (RACs) were taxed in a special way. Instead of using a tax code, basic rate tax of 22% was deducted automatically from the whole payment regardless of other income or what rate of tax you paid. As a result, many people ended up paying too much tax. They could claim it back each year, though many did not. If no tax was due on the RAC then a form called R89 could be signed so the pension was in future paid gross without tax being deducted. Again, many failed to fill in this form. Higher-rate taxpayers paid the extra tax due through their self-assessment form.

It was a rough and ready system and many of the 1.2 million people involved paid the wrong tax. So, from April 2007, RACs were brought into the PAYE system. In theory that is a good thing. It should have made sure the tax deducted was more accurate for everyone. But the changeover was managed very badly – many people were given the wrong code, the tax deducted was wrong, and the helpline went into meltdown.

Tax-saving tip: *If you receive a pension that you started paying into before 1 July 1988, make sure the tax now being deducted through PAYE is correct.*

People who had previously paid too much tax can reclaim the overpayment back to 2004/05 – and 2003/04 if they make the claim before 31 January 2010.

Tax-saving tip: *If you pay less tax under the new system, that probably means you have paid too much in the past. Consider claiming a refund – and do it before 31 January 2010.*

The State Pension and benefits

The State Pension is taxable but is paid without tax being deducted. So it uses up some of your tax-free personal allowance. The Revenue deducts it from your allowance to get your tax code. That makes it seem as if you are being taxed heavily on your earnings or private pension.

Even if you only have the State Pension you may have to pay tax, especially if you are a woman under 65 who gets the standard personal allowance. That is because the State Pension – including the earnings-related SERPS – may be enough by itself for tax to be due on it. If you have no other pension or earnings, then the tax will have to be paid through the self-assessment scheme (see pages 43–53).

Money-saving tip: *If you received Child Benefit for your children after April 1978, you may be entitled to Home Responsibilities Protection (HRP). That is a complicated way to give you a slightly higher pension for the time you spent caring for your children. Many women don't get the correct HRP allocated to them. Make sure the Department for Work and Pensions knows when you were getting Child Benefit and ask them to check that you are receiving the correct pension.*

The State Pension paid to a married woman aged 60 or more, whether based on her own contributions or her husband's, counts as her income. But if a married man gets extra State Pension for his wife who is under State Pension age, then that is taxed as part of his income.

Similar rules apply in the rare cases where a woman gets an Adult Dependency Increase for her husband. The Adult Dependency Increase will not be paid to people claiming for the first time from 6 April 2010.

> **Paul** *is 65 and his wife* **Mary** *is 59 and does not work. Because Mary is under 60, Paul claims an extra £57.05 on his pension for her. It is called an Adult Dependency Increase. This extra pension is taxed as his income. But once Mary reaches 60, this extra pension stops. At that point Mary can claim a pension on her own contributions, but she only has a very small amount due. So she claims a married woman's pension of £57.05 on Paul's National Insurance contributions. It is paid to her and is counted as her income when tax is worked out.*

If you think you may be entitled to this extra pension for a wife who is aged under 60, claim it before 6 April 2010.

Other taxable social security benefits (see pages 2–6), such as Bereavement Allowance or Incapacity Benefit (in some circumstances), may be less than your tax allowances, in which case no tax is due. But if you are liable for Income Tax, it will be collected by adjusting your tax code if you have another source of income such as an occupational pension. In rare cases where one of these benefits is more than your tax allowance by itself, it can be paid with the Income Tax already taken off.

Money-saving tip: *If you are a married woman, you may have paid some full contributions before you were married. That can entitle you to a pension in your own right, which you can claim at 60. If you worked between 1961 and 1975, you will also have earned some graduated retirement benefit (Graduated Pension) and work from April 1978 can entitle you to an earnings-related pension if you were paying full National Insurance contributions. Contact the Pension Service to make sure officials know about all your previous jobs and addresses so they can give you the correct pension.*

The Age Concern book Your Rights to Money Benefits *explains all about State pensions and benefits. If you want to contact the Pension Service, you can ring 0845 606 0265 and you will be connected to the pension centre covering your area, or look online at* www.thepensionservice.gov.uk

If you have a pension from abroad, the way it is taxed is very complex. A special concession means that only 90% of most foreign pensions is taxable in the UK. Normally, it will be paid gross though in some cases tax may already have been deducted by the country that pays it.

Tax-saving tip: *If you get a pension from abroad, get advice to make sure that only the correct amount of tax is deducted in the UK.*

Savings and investments

Interest paid on savings or investments is taxed in two different ways. Some interest is paid 'gross' – in other words, without tax being deducted first. If you pay tax, you will have to pay the tax on it later. But most interest and investment income is paid with the tax already deducted. Tax on dividends paid on shares is taxed in a peculiar way, explained on pages 32–33. Of course, some types of interest are tax free – they are listed on pages 2–6.

Interest paid gross

Some sorts of interest are paid gross. Interest from most taxable National Savings & Investments products is paid gross. But interest on Fixed Rate Savings Bonds is paid with tax already deducted. The interest paid on government stock, also called 'gilts', is paid gross unless you specifically ask for it to be paid net of tax. If you have money invested in a bank or building society outside the UK, then interest on that will normally be paid gross too.

Pain-saving tip: *Some people who were tempted by adverts to put money offshore to get the interest paid gross may think that means no tax was due. Sadly, it does not. The Revenue now has powers to track down offshore savings. So let the Revenue*

*know if you have undeclared money
abroad. It will be painful. But less painful
than if the Revenue catches you first.*

If your total income is too low for you to pay tax,
then you will not have to worry about paying tax
on income paid gross. But if you have to pay tax,
this will be done in one of two ways. If you pay tax
on earnings or a pension through PAYE and the
gross amount of interest you receive totals less
than £2,500, the tax on it can be collected through
your PAYE code. If not, you will be sent a self-
assessment tax form to account for the tax due
(see pages 43–53). If the tax is paid through your
tax code the amount collected is likely to be
approximate, so check at the end of the year that
the right amount has been taken.

Tax on interest

The basic rate of tax for income from savings is
20%. This rate applies to almost all types of
income from savings, including interest on bank
and building society accounts, taxable National
Savings products, and annuities that you purchase
as an investment, but not retirement annuities that
you have to buy with a pension fund, which are
taxed at the same rate as earnings.

But if your non-savings income (for example, income
from a pension or self-employment) is low – less than
£2,440 above your personal tax allowance – then
some of your savings income may be taxed at 10%.

- If your other (non-savings) income is more than
  £2,440 above your personal tax allowance, no
  savings interest is taxed at 10%.

- If your other income is less than your personal tax allowance, your savings interest will be tax free up to the point at which your other income combined with your savings income exceeds the amount of your allowance. Any savings income on top of that is taxed at 10%. No more than £2,440 of savings interest can be taxed at 10%; above this amount it is taxed at 20%.

- If your other income is less than £2,440 above your personal tax allowance, then subtract your personal allowance from your other income. Subtract that from £2,440. The answer is the maximum amount of savings interest that can be taxed at 10%.

For example, if your other income is £10,490 and your personal allowance is £9,490, subtract £9,490 from £10,490 to get £1,000. Subtract £1,000 from £2,440 to get £1,440. This is the maximum amount of savings interest that can be taxed at 10%.

If your income is high – above £43,875 in the year – you will normally have to pay higher-rate tax, which is 40%, on your savings income. As 20% will already have been deducted, you will have another 20% of the gross amount to pay.

Joint savings of husbands and wives

If a married couple or civil partners have savings or investments in their joint names, any income will normally be split equally when the tax is worked out. But if they own the savings or investment in unequal shares they can make a joint declaration setting out how it is owned. Each will then be taxed on their actual share of the income. It is only worth making the declaration if that will reduce the tax you pay. That will happen if the person who actually owns most of the income pays a lower rate of tax than the other partner.

Tax-saving tip: *A couple may be able to save tax by transferring savings to the partner who pays no tax or tax at a lower rate. (See the example of Sid and Lillian on pages 72–76.) If you do not want to transfer the money but have a joint account with a partner whose total income is too low to pay any tax, you should only pay tax on half the interest.*

Bank and building society accounts

Interest paid on money you have in a bank or building society account has basic rate tax of 20% deducted from it automatically. Even if you are not liable to pay tax, or liable to pay it only at the 10% rate on some savings income, the bank or building society will deduct tax at the full 20% without asking you. It's not their fault: it's the law!

If your income is too low for you to pay tax, then you can apply for the interest to be paid gross – without tax being deducted. So if you expect your total gross income for the year to be less than your tax allowances, apply to have the interest paid gross.

You do this by completing form R85, which is available from your bank or building society, a tax office or online at *www.hmrc.gov.uk/forms/r85.pdf*.

You will need to fill in a separate form for each of your accounts. If you have a joint account, then any account holder who is a non-taxpayer can fill in the form. For example, if the husband pays tax and the wife does not, then half the interest can be paid tax free.

Tax-saving tip: *Check your bank and building society accounts to see how much tax has been deducted. If too much has been taken off, you can get it back for up to six tax years using form R40 – you will need one form for each year for which you are claiming tax back and one each if you have joint savings. You can download the form at www.hmrc.gov.uk/forms/r40.pdf. Don't worry if it has the wrong date printed on it. Just cross it out and write in the tax year to which it applies.*

Even if you are liable to pay tax only at the 10% rate on some or all of your savings interest, the full 20% rate will be deducted and you will have to claim back the tax that has been overpaid. Similarly, if you are a non-taxpayer but you have not asked the bank or building society to pay the interest gross, then you will have to apply for a refund of any tax overpaid. You can make an application if you have overpaid tax in the last six years; back to the year 2003/04 (although for that year you have to apply by 31 January 2010).

Falling interest rates mean that the income from savings is much lower in 2009/10 than it was in earlier years. That may bring your total income below the level at which tax is due or it may mean

that tax is due on it at only 10%. So it is very important to check your position in 2009/10.

Dividend income

If you own shares, you will normally be paid a dividend once or twice a year. These dividends are taxed in a peculiar way. You will be sent the money net of basic rate tax. But the basic rate on dividends is only 10%. So if your dividend is £100, you will be sent £90 (£100 minus £10), and the document that accompanies the cheque will also show what is called a 'tax credit' of £10, showing you have paid £10 tax. If your income is not high enough to pay tax, you cannot claim back this £10. Keep this document as part of your tax records.

If you have to pay higher-rate tax, then you will have to pay extra tax on the dividends you have received in the tax year. Your gross dividend income will be taxed at the rate of 32.5%. As you have already paid 10%, you will owe a further 22.5% on the gross dividend, which is 25% of the net dividend. You can work out the gross amount of the dividend by adding up the amount you got and the tax credit. Even if you do not pay higher-rate tax, you may need to work out the grossed-up amount to see if you are entitled to the higher tax allowances for people aged 65 or more (see pages 9–12).

Unit trusts and OEICs

The income from unit trusts or open-ended investment companies (OEICs) can be paid either as interest or as dividends. If it is paid as interest – often called an 'interest distribution' – it is treated like interest on money in a bank or building society. Tax will be deducted at 20% before you are paid the interest. If it is paid as a dividend, it is taxed like dividends.

ISAs and PEPs

Individual Savings Accounts (ISAs) were introduced in 1999 as a new way of tax-free saving. ISAs are not investments in themselves. They are simply a way of labelling savings or investments to show they are tax free.

Until 5 October 2009 you can put up to £3,600 into a cash ISA in 2009/10. But from 6 October the limit rises to £5,100 for anyone aged 50 or more. If you are 50 after 6 October but before 6 April 2010, you can put in the extra on your 50th birthday. The cash ISA limit for 2010/11 will be £5,100 for people of any age. The total ISA limit also rises in the same way from £7,200 to £10,200. ISA limit for 2009/10 is £7,200.

The balance on top of any cash ISA can be put into an ISA invested in shares or other things like bonds or gilts. Alternatively, you can put the whole amount into investments – but not into cash. The interest earned is tax free and no Capital Gains Tax is paid on any gain. If the money is invested in shares, then the automatic 10% tax is still taken off any dividends. So shares ISAs are mainly of benefit to higher-rate taxpayers. In some circumstances if your income is around the limit where age allowance runs out, the dividends on a shares ISA may help you avoid losing your age allowance. And in rare cases where you have capital gains over £10,100, shares ISAs may help avoid CGT.

PEPs – Personal Equity Plans – were an earlier form of tax-free stock market investment. No new money could be put in them from April 1999 and they have been renamed ISAs from April 2008.

Other investment income

If you have purchased an annuity as an investment rather than as part of a pension plan, only part of the money you get each month is treated as income – the rest is treated as a return of your capital and is not taxed. The income part is normally paid with 20% tax automatically deducted.

If your income is below your tax allowances, or you are only due to pay tax at the 10% rate, you can claim back some or all of this tax. If you are due to pay tax at the higher rate, then you will have to pay extra tax on this income. Only the part treated as income is counted when you work out your entitlement to age-related tax allowances.

The Revenue says it is keen to help people claim back tax they may have overpaid on savings and investments. There is a helpline for claiming tax back on 0845 366 7850. Or call 0845 980 0645 about registering to have your interest paid gross. Calls are charged at local rates. There is also a useful booklet, IR111: Bank and building society interest: Are you paying tax when you don't need to? *which is available on the Revenue website at* www.hmrc.gov.uk/leaflets/ir111.pdf. *There is also information about reclaiming tax at* www.hmrc.gov.uk/taxback. *The Revenue*

is planning a major taxback campaign aimed at people over 60 in the autumn of 2009. It says people on pension credit could be owed an average of £200 each.

What are tax codes?

A tax code normally consists of a number followed by a letter. The number represents the amount of money you can have tax free in the year, with the last digit removed.

£ So if your tax allowance for 2009/10 was £6,475, your code would start 647. Your employer then knows to allow you £6,479 during the year without taking any tax off.

The last figure is always a '9' to try to make sure the code system errs on your side: in other words, your allowance is slightly higher than the £6,475 it should be.

In 2008/09 tax codes were made more complex because the personal allowance was changed during the year. So the tax deducted was reduced from September. No such complexity is anticipated in 2009/10.

The code number is followed by a letter that shows what kind of allowance you have. A common code for people under 65 is 647L. The 'L' stands for lower personal allowance – there isn't a lower personal allowance any more but quite a lot of things in tax codes are hangovers from the past.

One thing that confuses people is that their State Pension is taxable – but it is paid in full without tax taken off. If you have other income from earnings or another pension, then the Revenue collects the tax due on the State Pension by deducting it from your tax allowance.

The common letters used in tax codes are:

- **L** – you get the personal allowance for people under 65.

- **P** – you get the full personal allowance for someone aged 65 to 74.

- **Y** – you get the full personal allowance for someone aged 75 or over.

> **Irene** *is 70 and has a State Pension of £97.50 a week, which is £5,070 a year. Irene's age is between 65 and 74, so her tax allowance is £9,490. She takes her State Pension from her allowance to give £4,420 and knocks off the last digit to give 442. She checks her code and sees it is 442P. The 'P' means she gets the full higher personal allowance for someone aged 65–74. The code means that this year she is allowed £4,429 on top of her State Pension before tax is due. So if her other income is £369 a month or less, then she will pay no tax on it.*

If you had a tax code ending in 'V' then it will be changed in 2009/10 as the V code is no longer being used. In 2009/10 you will reach the age of 75 and will be entitled to the higher tax allowance for those over 75 of £9,640 and to the married couple's allowance. Your code will probably end in a 'T'.

- **K** – if your pension is more than your tax allowance, then you will be given a K code. You get a K code when untaxed income, such as the State Pension or gross interest from savings, exceeds your personal allowances. The 'K' comes before the digits and means that you have a 'negative' allowance – in other words, instead of deducting an amount from your income before tax is worked out, extra income is added and tax worked out on the total. The amount to add is divided by 10 and rounded down to the nearest whole number and then placed after the K. That means the actual income you have is taxed at a higher rate than normal. But you will never have tax deducted at more than 50% from any one source of your income. If it is not possible to collect all the tax due because of this restriction, then you will be placed in the self-assessment system.

Myra *is 62. She has worked all her life and has paid full National Insurance contributions for most of that time. Her State Pension – which includes a lot of SERPS – is now £142 a week (£7,384 a year). But as she is 62, her tax allowance was only £6,475 at the start of the year. So she has to pay tax on £909 of her pension. As she is still in work that is done by adding that amount on to her earnings before the tax is worked out. The £909 is divided by ten and rounded down to 90 and her tax code is K90.*

Other codes you might see are:

- **T** – is used if your age-related personal allowance is reduced because your income is above the income limit of £22,900. You will also get a 'T' code if you have asked the tax office not to reveal to your employer or pension payer what your circumstances are.
- **0T** – is a variation of the T code and indicates that there is no tax allowance and all the income is to be taxed at the basic rate.
- **BR** – tax is to be collected at the basic rate on all of this source of income. This code might be used if you have more than one source of income. The tax allowance is normally included in the tax code for your main source of income and so tax is due on all other sources of income.
- **D0** – means all the income from this job or pension is to be taxed at the higher rate of 40%. That might happen if you had several sources of income which in total were well above £43,875 in 2009/10.
- **NT** – no tax is to be deducted – a rare but welcome code!

If you reach 65 or 75 during the tax year, then the Revenue will not include the higher tax allowance as part of your tax code automatically. That is not a mistake – it is a policy! The Revenue prefers to wait until the following tax year and then adjust that tax code to refund any tax overpaid. But if you insist, it will change your tax code in good time.

Tax-saving tip: *If your 65th or 75th birthday is due in 2009/10, tell the Revenue now and say you want the correct allowance at once.*

Notice of Coding

The Revenue used to issue a Notice of Coding to everyone on PAYE each year. Employees now no longer get this service if their circumstances remain the same each year. But if you are on PAYE and you have a State Pension or other amounts deducted from your code, then you should get a Notice of Coding – called a P2 – each year, normally in January or February, so you can check it. It will show your tax code and how it is worked out.

The Revenue used to include with it a useful leaflet called *Understanding your tax code*. But it has stopped producing it – instead the Notice of Coding P2 should contain notes and information that explain how your tax code is worked out. It also tells you the tax office to contact if you think the coding is wrong.

You can read more about tax codes on the Revenue website at www.hmrc.gov.uk/incometax/understand-p2.htm

If you have more than one source of income taxed through PAYE, you should have a tax code (and a Notice of Coding) for each. But your allowances will normally be used for the biggest source of income. The other sources may have a 0T, BR or D0 code. Check that the figures are correct and that the calculation makes sense. A recent report by the National Audit Office found that having multiple sources of income makes it, "more difficult for the Department to ensure the right amount of tax is collected during the year and that all the necessary information is brought together at the end of the year to check the accuracy of deductions". So it is very important to check your code.

When you get a new Notice of Coding, check that:

- you have been given the correct allowances – on at least one of your income sources:
- the deductions for the State Pension and any untaxed investment income are correct;
- the addition and subtraction are right; and
- the code letter is the appropriate one for your circumstances.

If you disagree with anything on the Notice of Coding, take a copy of it and send the original back to the tax office, saying what you think is wrong. Alternatively, you can phone your tax office to find out more or to request that a change be made.

Code changes

There may be changes in your circumstances that affect your code. For example:

- If you get a new source of income – perhaps you start a new job or self-employment, or you start drawing a pension – then your tax code may not cope with the change. If you change jobs, the employer you leave should give you a form for your new employer called a P45, which shows your tax code. Until they get that P45 your earnings will normally be taxed on an 'emergency code'. That may mean you pay too much tax.

- In some circumstances you will start a job and not have a P45 – that might happen if you retired from a job, got an occupational pension, and then took up a new job. If you do not have a P45, your new employer should ask you to sign form P46 and give you form P15 (allowances claim) so that the right PAYE code can be obtained for taxing your earnings.

It is up to you to inform the tax office of any changes that might affect your code and the amount of tax you pay. But even if you do not, remember that the code is only a way of collecting the tax, not of assessing it. If you end up paying too much, you can claim it back – and if you pay too little, the Revenue can demand it from you later.

If your code does change – apart from the change when the personal allowance goes up each year – you should be notified by the Revenue. If the number in the code goes up, you will be paying less tax through PAYE; if it goes down, you will be paying more – it's the opposite way round with the K code, of course.

What can go wrong?

The simple answer to that question is – a lot. Here are just some of the things that can go wrong that help the Revenue deduct £500 million too much each year:

- **The amount of your State Pension changes in April** and the Department for Work and Pensions (DWP) should automatically provide information to the Revenue about how much it is. Sometimes, though, the two government departments cannot match up the data and the Revenue is not told exactly how much your pension is. In that case it will work out your new pension from last year's figure. But that calculation is approximate and may be wrong. So always check that the correct amount of pension has been taken into account. If the amount of your State Pension has been overestimated, contact your tax office to explain; otherwise you will pay too much tax.

- If you have any untaxed investment income – such as the interest on government stock (gilts – see page 89) or from offshore savings – then an estimated amount for that may be deducted from your allowance. Remember this is an estimate. If the actual amount is different, then the wrong tax will have been deducted throughout the year. So always check.

> **Ross** has some government stock which earned him £400 last year in interest paid in two lots of £200. He has to pay tax at 20% on that, which is £80. So the Revenue reduces his tax code by 40. That increases the tax he pays on his other income by £400 x 20%, which is £80. However, next year his gilt comes to an end and only one £200 payment is due. So he pays £80 tax when he should only pay £40. He has to claim a refund of the rest.

- Married Couple's Allowance is a fixed amount deducted from your Income Tax, rather than being an allowance in the normal sense, and it cannot easily be taken account of in a tax code. But the Revenue tries to do just that. If you get Married Couple's Allowance, it will be added to your allowances but then an amount will be taken off it – called an allowance restriction – to try to make sure the tax is right. But it may give the wrong answer and you should check at the end of the tax year to see if the correct tax has been deducted. In some cases the Revenue does not impose the restriction and that can lead to too little tax being paid. Visit *www.direct.gov.uk* for more information.

If you get the Married Couple's Allowance and your spouse dies, or you stop living together permanently or divorce (or dissolve a civil partnership), then the allowance will normally cease from the following tax year. Make sure that is reflected in your code or you may end up paying too little tax.

How does self-assessment work?

More than a million pensioners pay their tax through the system called self-assessment. If you are one of them in 2009/10, you should have been sent a tax return in April 2009. This form relates to your income and allowances for 2008/09.

There are two different deadlines for getting the form back.

- If you do it online you have until 31 January 2010 – though beware that as the date approaches the website can get very busy and slow.

- If you do not want to do it online you have to get the paper form back by 31 October 2009. The Revenue will then work out the tax you have to pay and let you know the amount in time for you to pay it before the payment deadline, which is 31 January 2010.

If you miss the 31 October paper deadline you can still register for online filing and meet the 31 January deadline. But if you miss that deadline you will have to pay a penalty of £100 (though if the tax you are due to pay is less than that the penalty cannot be more than the tax due).

Registering to deal with it online is relatively easy. Go to the *www.hmrc.gov.uk* website and click on 'self-assessment' on the green panel on the left. Once you have filled in the details, the Revenue will post you a PIN. You will need to use that to complete the process online within 28 days or you will have to start the process again.

The online service is safe and secure. It works out the tax you owe, and you get a receipt for the form once you have submitted it. (If you post the paper form or deliver it personally to a local Revenue office, you do not get a receipt.)

If you have to pay tax for 2008/09, it will be due on 31 January 2010. You may also have to make payments on account for 2009/10 (see pages 47–49). If you miss these deadlines, you may be subject to penalties and interest.

Whom does it affect?

Most older people do not need to worry about self-assessment. But it may affect you if:

- you are self-employed, a partner in a business or a company director;
- you pay higher-rate tax;
- you are a minister of religion;
- you are over 65 and your income is above £22,900;
- your only income is the State Pension and interest that is not taxed at source;
- you have untaxed income from investments (though if you are old enough to get State Pension and this can be collected through PAYE, then you will need to fill in a different form called P810); or
- you have rental income from letting a property outside the rent-a-room scheme.

Most older people who pay tax on their pension or earnings through PAYE, and whose savings interest has tax deducted from it before it is paid, will not be sent a tax return and need not worry about self-assessment.

But even if your income is quite low, you may still be sent a tax return if you have untaxed income that cannot be collected through PAYE.

If you have less than £2,500 of income that is not taxed at source and you have a PAYE code, then the tax will automatically be collected by adjusting your code.

You can opt out of this system by filling in a box – this year page TR5, box 2 – on your self-assessment return.

Filling in the form

The self-assessment tax returns are sent out after 5 April and ask for information about your income in the previous tax year. The basic tax form may contain extra pages covering sources of income such as employment, self-employment or rental income. There will also be a guide to completing the form and an extra couple of short forms that you need to fill in only if you have to. The forms can seem very complicated, so allow yourself plenty of time and ask for help if necessary.

You may be able to get help from a local advice agency and there are two charities that will give you free help with tax. They are listed on page 122. Alternatively, you can ask the Revenue or pay an accountant or tax adviser to help you.

About one in three older people who have to fill in a self-assessment form will be sent a simpler four-page version called the Short Tax Return. You cannot apply to have the short form – if you get the long one, you must complete it – and if you are sent the short one, you have to check that you are eligible for it. Although the form is short, it comes with a lengthy guide. The first two pages help you to decide whether or not the form is suitable for you. The short form does not allow you to work out precisely how much tax you owe. It has to be filled in and sent back by 31 October or you will face a penalty. The Revenue will tell you the tax you are due to pay by 31 January 2010.

If you are not usually sent a tax return but have a new source of income or a capital gain on which you need to pay tax, you must tell the Revenue by 5 October after the end of the tax year – so if you had a new source of income in 2008/09, you must tell the Revenue by 5 October 2009. You will then be sent a tax return to complete. Check when it has to be returned by.

When is tax paid?

Income Tax is charged on income received in the current tax year. The tax is due on 31 January and 31 July, with any balance due the following 31 January. In other words, at the end of January 2010 you are expected to pay half the tax due on income from 6 April 2009 to 5 April 2010. That is clearly impossible to do accurately, as you may not know exactly how much your income will be between 1 February and 5 April. So the tax you pay is always an estimate and the payments you make are called 'on account'. (No payment on account has to be made if the tax due is less than £1,000.) The tax paid is corrected in the following year from the information in your next tax return.

The timetable runs like this:

• **April 2009** – tax returns are sent out for the tax year 2008/09. You complete yours with the details of your income and allowances for 2008/09. That information is used to calculate exactly the tax that was due in 2008/09. You may have already made payments of this tax in January and July 2008.

- **31 October 2009** – deadline for paper forms to be sent back. The Revenue will calculate the tax due in 2008/09 and the estimated amount of the tax due in 2009/10 in time for the payment to be made by 31 January 2010. If you return a paper form later than 31 October the Revenue will still calculate the tax but may not do so in time for the January deadline – in which case, you have to work this out yourself.

- **31 January 2010** – deadline for online filing of the form. If you have missed the paper deadline you can file online by this date. A penalty of £100 (less if your tax is less than that) will be imposed if you miss this final deadline. Half the estimated tax for 2009/10 is due (this is called a payment on account). In addition, any overpayment or underpayment for 2008/09 is corrected. If there was an underpayment, a further payment is due. If there has been an overpayment, then a refund is due. Normally, the extra money or the refund is simply added on or taken off the tax due on account for 2009/10.

If the balancing payment for 2008/09 is less than £2,000, it can be collected through PAYE in a future year, but only if you get your tax return back by 31 October 2009 (on paper or online). If your income goes down significantly from one year to the next, then your estimated tax is likely to be more than the amount actually due. If your circumstances change in this way, you can tell the Revenue and pay less on account.

Ask for a form SA303 or download it at:
www.hmrc.gov.uk/sa/forms/sa303.pdf

But if it turns out you got it wrong and you pay too little tax, you will be charged interest on the unpaid tax back to the date it was due.

What records have to be kept?

All taxpayers are obliged by law to keep records of their income and capital gains. Unless you are self-employed (see pages 77–87) or rent out property (except under the rent-a-room scheme – see page 4), you can normally destroy records for 2007/08 – in other words, those relating to your affairs up to 5 April 2008 – on 1 February 2010. You may have to keep your records longer if:

- the tax return was late;
- there is an enquiry going on into your tax affairs; or
- your tax return was sent to you late in the year.

If you are self-employed or have rental income, the deadline for destroying documents is normally a minimum of five years later (see pages 83–84).

What penalties are there?

If you are sent a form, you must complete it. If you do not, you could face a penalty. If you use the paper form it must be back by 31 October 2009. If you miss that deadline the Revenue will not work out how much tax you owe in time for the payment deadline of 31 January 2010 so you will have to work the tax out yourself. If you use the online service (and you can choose to do that after the paper deadline has passed) you must complete your form online by 31 January 2010. If you miss that date there is an automatic penalty of £100 – though it cannot be more than the tax that is due, so if you owe no tax no penalty will be imposed. You must also pay the tax owed by 31 January. If you pay the tax after that date, you may incur interest and surcharges on any tax paid late.

However, if you are self-employed or run a small business and would have difficulty paying your tax because of the recession and credit crisis the Revenue will allow you to negotiate later payment of your tax. It is called Business Payment Support and you can find out more from the Revenue at www.hmrc.gov.uk/pbr2008/business-payment.htm or by calling 0845 302 1435. Business Payment Support began on 24 November 2008. No end date has been announced though it should continue as long as the recession affects businesses. You should always ask for help before your tax is due.

The key dates for tax returns for 2008/09 are:

- **April 2009** – tax returns for 2008/09 are sent out by the Revenue to people it thinks need to fill one in.
- **31 October 2009** – if you do not return your paper form by this date, the Revenue will not guarantee to calculate your tax by the time it is due. If your form misses this date, you will not be able to arrange to pay extra tax due through the PAYE system. If you send back a paper form later than this you will be charged a penalty of £100 (or the amount of tax due if that is less).

If you miss the paper deadline, register to submit the form online and do it by 31 January 2010.

- **31 January 2010** – if you are submitting your form online, you must do so by this date. The penalty for missing this date is normally £100 (but if you owe less tax than £100, the penalty cannot be more than the tax that is due). If you do not owe any tax or you have a reasonable excuse for your return being late, you will not have to pay the penalty. Some people are sent penalties by mistake. So always consider appealing against a penalty. There may also be a daily fine of £60 for each day the form is late, but this is rarely imposed.

- **31 January 2010** – a balancing payment for 2008/09 is due, and so is the payment on account for the tax year 2009/10. Interest is charged on unpaid tax for every day it is late. From January 2009 this rate is 4.5% a year.

- **28 February 2010** – a 5% surcharge is added onto any tax due for 2008/09 that has still not been paid unless you have agreed a payment deferral under the Business Payment Support scheme.

- **28 March 2010** – if a surcharge was due and it has not been paid, interest begins to be charged on the surcharge.

- **31 July 2010** – if your tax return has still not been submitted on paper or online, a second £100 penalty is imposed.

- **31 July 2010** – a further 5% surcharge is added to any tax due for 2008/09 that has still not been paid unless you have agreed a payment deferral under the Business Payment Support scheme.

- **28 August 2010** – if the further surcharge was due and has not been paid, interest begins to be charged on it.

For further information, help or leaflets, contact the Self-Assessment Team at your tax office (the telephone number is at the top of your return). In the evenings and at weekends you can call the Revenue's Self-Assessment Helpline on 0845 9000 444. Or check out the website at www.hmrc.gov.uk/sa/forms/content.htm

After you send in your tax return

If you have sent in a paper return you will be sent a Tax Calculation. You should check that the figures are correct, as mistakes are often made. If you want to amend anything, let the Revenue know as soon as possible.

Everyone who is sent a tax return has a 'tax account' opened at the Revenue. You will receive a Statement of Account once a year showing the money you owe. You will also receive one in certain other circumstances, including:

- when there are changes to items in your account;
- when a tax payment is due in the next 35 days;
- every two months when between £32 and £500 is due;

- every month when over £500 is due;
- when the Revenue has arranged for unpaid tax to be collected through PAYE; or
- when you have paid more tax than is due.

 Check your Statement of Account when you receive it, and contact the Revenue if you disagree with the entries. A small number of tax returns are selected for investigation – they are called 'enquiries'. Usually this is because something appears wrong or the figures have changed significantly from one year to the next. But a few tax returns are selected at random.

 Tax-saving tip: *Even if you submit a paper form by 31 October and the Revenue works out your tax, check it. The Revenue admits that it gets around half a million self-assessment calculations wrong each year. You can claim back any tax that has been overpaid.*

Who has to pay National Insurance contributions?

If you work and earn £110 a week or more, you will have to pay National Insurance contributions. They will normally be deducted from your pay before you get it. But the last week you have to pay them is the week before you reach State Pension age – currently 60 for a woman, 65 for a man. From April 2010, pension age for women will

slowly rise. Check your pension age at
*www.thepensionservice.gov.uk/state-pension/
age-calculator.asp*

Tax-saving tip: *Once you reach 60 or 65,
check that no National Insurance
contributions are being deducted from
your pay. They should stop with the last
payment before your birthday.*

If you are self-employed and are below State
Pension age, then you may have to pay two
separate National Insurance contributions – they
are called Class 2 and Class 4:

- **Class 2 contributions** are £2.40 a week in the
  2009/10 tax year. If you reach State Pension
  age during a tax year your last Class 2 has to
  be paid in the week before you reach that age.
  Class 2 contributions are paid quarterly, or
  when you are sent a bill, or by monthly direct
  debit. Revenue leaflet SE1 includes a direct
  debit mandate you can use. You will be exempt
  from Class 2 contributions if you expect your
  annual profit to be below £5,075. It is called
  'small earnings exception' and must be
  claimed in advance. In practice the Revenue
  may agree to backdate an application. Class 2
  contributions count towards your State
  Pension.

Download the form at
www.hmrc.gov.uk/forms/cf10.pdf *and
send it off as soon as you can.*

- **Class 4 contributions** are collected by the Revenue with your Income Tax. Contributions are charged at 8% on profits between £5,715 and £43,875 in 2009/10 and at 1% on profits above that. You have to pay Class 4 contributions for the whole tax year in which you reach State Pension age, but not after that. Class 4 contributions do not help you qualify for a State Pension or other benefits. They are simply a tax.

If you have income from paid employment as well as from self-employment, and you are under State Pension age, you will be paying **Class 1 contributions**, which are deducted straight from your earnings. If you are due to pay Class 1 and Class 2 contributions there are complex rules that fix a maximum amount of National Insurance contributions you have to pay and your Class 2 and Class 4 contributions may be reduced. If this is likely to apply to you, seek advice from the National Insurance Contributions Office (see page 121).

Tax-saving tip: *If you are employed or self-employed, check that you are not paying too much in National Insurance contributions.*

For more information, see the Revenue website at www.hmrc.gov.uk/nic/class2.htm *and* www.hmrc.gov.uk/nic/class4.htm

Married women's reduced-rate contributions

It is not often that this book recommends paying more tax. But one group of working women should consider doing so. If you are under 60, married and have been in work fairly continuously since before May 1977, then you may still be paying the reduced-rate married women's National Insurance contributions.

These contributions earn you nothing. They do not count towards a State Pension. And in some cases they can stop you paying extra contributions to boost your State Pension. They are a complete waste of money.

Unfortunately, the only way to stop paying them is to change to the full contributions. That will cost you more but they earn you rights to the State Pension and count towards the earnings-related State Second Pension (which used to be called SERPS). For most women aged under 59 it is better to change. You can do that at any time during the tax year on form CF9. The only group who may gain nothing from changing at the moment are those who pay into salary-related company pension schemes and who have a very small entitlement to their own State Pension.

For more information, see www.hmrc.gov.uk/faqs/women_reduced_rate.htm *and for the form to fill in see* www.hmrc.gov.uk/forms/cf9.pdf

Overpaid contributions

If you have paid too much in National Insurance contributions, you can claim the excess back. There are several reasons why you might pay too much – for example:

- you stopped being self-employed;
- you were working or self-employed after reaching State Pension age;
- your earnings were below £110 a week;
- you had more than one job;
- you were employed and self-employed at the same time; or
- you qualified for the small earnings exception but did not apply.

Most overpaid National Insurance contributions can only be reclaimed for the last six tax years. But if you paid too much in contributions because you have more than one job or you earned below the threshold and should not have paid contributions at all, you can reclaim the overpayment without any time limit.

If you think you have overpaid, apply in writing to HM Revenue & Customs, NICO, Benton Park View, Newcastle upon Tyne NE98 1ZZ. Send them any evidence you have and explain which contributions you think you have overpaid. Always include your National Insurance number.

How to check your tax bill

Even the Revenue admits that many people pay too much or too little tax. PAYE, self-assessment and the automatic deduction of tax from interest are all responsible for the wrong tax being paid. People with more than one source of income and people who reach 65 or 75 during the tax year are also often charged the wrong tax.

This section of the book shows you how to check that you are paying the right amount of Income Tax. If you follow the steps below, you will find out whether you should pay tax at all and, if so, how much you are due to pay. You will need a calculator, paper and pen, as well as a logical approach. There are questions in each step. Answer them 'yes' or 'no' and then follow the appropriate instruction.

If you are told to go to another step, go straight there. Otherwise, carry on with the step you are on. Some steps tell you to write down the tax so far and give it a name such as 'Tax (B)'. It is best to circle or highlight these amounts because you will need them later.

Your income comes in three types. Each type can be taxed differently. First, there are dividends paid on shares or investments. Most people don't have any dividends. But if you do, they sit right on the very top of your income – like a layer of thick double cream. Second, there is interest earned on savings. That forms the middle layer of your income – like the single cream. Quite a lot of people will have savings interest. Third, there is all the rest of your taxable income – that will normally be from pensions and earnings but also includes profits from self-employment or from rent if you let out a property. All that income sits at the bottom – like the milk under the cream and double cream.

Tax allowances and rates of tax are applied from the bottom of these layers up. So the allowances or the tax rate applies first to your income from earnings, pension or rent, then to your savings interest and then to any dividends. Because each of these three kinds of income is taxed differently, the calculation can be complex. But most people can skip a lot of the steps and the arithmetic should not be that difficult. It is mainly adding and subtracting!

Step 1 – Income

List your income separately in three columns:

Column A – non-investment income. That includes pensions (state, company and personal), earnings, self-employment profits and rent (after expenses) if you let out property.

Column B – interest on savings in a bank or building society.

Column C – dividends.

Delete all the income that is tax free (see pages 2–6). Don't worry if some columns contain zero. That just makes your calculation simpler!

Make sure that all the remaining income is listed gross (in other words, before tax is deducted). For income that you receive tax paid, such as interest on money in a bank or building society, gross it up by dividing by 4 and multiplying by 5. Gross up dividend income by dividing by 9 and multiplying by 10. Add up each column (A, B and C) separately to get total A, total B and total C.

Step 2 – Personal Tax Allowance

Were you born on 6 April 1945 or later?

- **Yes:** Your personal tax allowance is £6,475. If you are blind, add £1,890 to make £8,365.

Write down your personal tax allowance and call it 'P'.

P = £_____

Go to Step 3.

- **No:** Sorry – you have a bit more calculating to do. If you made any Gift Aid donations (see page 19) gross them up by dividing by 4 and multiplying by 5. Call that 'G'.

If you made any pension contributions of any sort, gross all of them up the same way and call that 'N'.

Add up A, B and C and then take away G and N so you get A+B+C–G–N. Call that 'total income' – the inverted commas indicate it is not really your total income, just a technical term used by HMRC needed in this step only.

Look up your personal allowance on page 117. If you are aged 65 or over and your 'total income' is less than £22,900, you can claim the full personal tax allowance for your age. If it is more than £22,900, reduce the allowance by £1 for every £2 of income above £22,900. But do not reduce your personal tax allowance below £6,475. If you are blind, add on the £1,890 Blind Person's

Allowance. Do not add on the Married Couple's Allowance, even if you are entitled to it. That is dealt with at Step 10. (Allowances are explained on pages 117–119.) Write down your personal tax allowance and call it 'P'.

P = £_____

If P = £6,475 (or £8,365 if you are blind), go to Step 3. Otherwise go to Step 8.

Step 3 – Dividend income

Do you have any dividend income?

- **No:** Breathe a sigh of relief and skip to Step 6.
- **Yes:** Things may get complicated for you. Go to Step 4.

Step 4 – Is there extra tax to pay on your dividend income?

Add your personal tax allowance P and £37,400. Now, separately, add A and B and C.

Is A+B+C bigger than P+£37,400?

- **No:** There is no extra tax due on your dividends. Breathe a bigger sigh of relief and skip to Step 6.
- **Yes:** Things are about to become complicated. Go to Step 5.

Step 5 – How much tax is due on your dividend income?

This is quite a complicated step.

Add A and B.
Add P and £37,400.

Is A+B bigger than P+£37,400?

- **Yes:** Multiply C by 0.225. Call this Tax (D). Go to Step 6.
- **No:** Add A+B+C, subtract £37,400 and subtract P. Multiply the answer by 0.225. Call this Tax (D). Go to Step 8.

Step 6 – Do you pay higher-rate tax?

Add A and B.
Add P and £37,400.

Is A+B bigger than P+£37,400?

- **Yes:** Add A and B and subtract P, then subtract £37,400.

A+B–P–£37,400 = £_____

Multiply the result by 0.4. Call this Tax (H). Go to Step 7.

- **No:** You have no higher-rate tax to pay. Go to Step 8.

Step 7 – Remaining income

You have arrived here because you paid some higher-rate tax. Now you must reduce your income by the amount that has been taxed at the higher rate before going to the next step.

Is A bigger than P+£37,400?

- **Yes:** Make B = 0. Make A = P+£37,400. Go to Step 9.
- **No:** Make B = P+£37,400–A. Don't change A. Go to Step 9.

Step 8 – Do you pay basic rate tax?

Is A+B bigger than P?

- **Yes:** You have to pay some basic rate tax. Go to Step 9.
- **No:** You have no basic rate tax to pay. If you have written down some Tax (D) (from Step 5) then go to Step 10. Otherwise, go to Step 11. You have no tax to pay.

Step 9 – How much basic rate tax?

If you have come here from Step 7, remember to use your amended income figures for A and B. Just to check: A+B should now equal P+£37,400. If you have come here from Step 8 then A+B will always be less than £37,400.

Add A and B and subtract P.
A+B–P = £_____
Multiply the result by 0.2. Call this number 'Z'.
Add P to £2,440.
P+£2,440 = £_____

Is A bigger than P+£2,440?

- **Yes:** Z is your basic rate tax. Call it Tax (B). Go to Step 10.
- **No:** It's going to get complicated. Take Z and go to Step 9a.

Step 9a – Reducing the tax for the starting rate for savings

This is the trickiest step of all. Once you have answered **'Yes'** or **'No'** to the first question, that leads to another question which also has to be answered **'Yes'** or **'No'**.

Is A bigger than P?

- **No:** Then answer the following question:

Is Z bigger than £488? Yes, Z is bigger than £488: Subtract £244 from Z. Call the answer Tax (B). Go to Step 10. No, Z is not bigger than £488: Divide Z by 2. Call the answer Tax (B). Go to Step 10.

- **Yes:** Then answer the following question:

Is Z bigger than £488? Yes, Z is bigger than £488: Add P to £2,440 and subtract A. Multiply the answer by 0.1. Subtract it from Z. Call the answer Tax (B). Go to Step 10. No, Z is not bigger than £488: Multiply B by 0.1 and subtract it from Z. Call the answer Tax (B). Go to Step 10.

Step 10 – Married Couple's Allowance

If you are at this step, you will have some tax to pay so far. It could be Tax (B), Tax (H) or Tax (D) or a combination of them. Add up whichever of these three numbers you have written down earlier. Call the total 'Y'.

Are you entitled to any Married Couple's Allowance?

If you are not sure, see pages 13–17. To get Married Couple's Allowance, at least one spouse must have been born before 6 April 1935.

- **No:** Y is the tax you should have paid in 2009/10. Call it 'T'. Go to Step 11.
- **Yes:** A bit more arithmetic to do.

Use pages 13–17 to work out your Married Couple's Allowance. There are some tricky bits to check. Do you give any of it to your spouse? Is your total income above the £29,230 limit to get the full allowance? If so, remember to reduce it according to the rules.

Whatever your MCA is, divide it by 10. Call this number 'M'.

Is Y bigger than M?

- **Yes:** Subtract M from Y. The answer is the amount of tax you should pay in 2009/10. Call it 'T'. Take this figure to Step 11.
- **No:** You should pay no tax in 2009/10. Call your tax zero and take this figure to Step 11.

Step 11

By the time you get here, you should have one figure for tax due. That is the tax you should have paid in 2009/10. That figure might, of course, be zero.

Now you must check if you have already paid too much tax. Add up the tax that has been deducted from the interest paid on a bank or building society account. You will find that in your statements or your paying-in book.

If the tax you have paid is bigger than the tax you are due to pay, then you are due some tax back. Apply for a refund. And there may be refunds due for the last six tax years as well.

If it is smaller, deduct it from the tax due. This is the amount of tax you still have to pay. Now check how much tax has been deducted from earnings or a pension through PAYE. If it is more than the tax due, apply for a refund.

Well done! You have worked out if you should Pay Less Tax!

EXAMPLES

1. Single person

Joan, 77, gets the Basic State Pension, which includes some Graduated Retirement Benefit and a tiny bit of SERPS. It totals £101.10 a week. She also has a small pension from her former employer of £220 a month gross. Joan relies on the interest from her savings of £60,000 to give her a reasonable income. Last year the interest was 5%, bringing her in £200 a month after tax. But this year the rate has halved and she gets just £100 a month or £1,200 over the year. She grosses that up by multiplying by 5 and dividing by 4, which is £1,500 gross. She gets the money each month minus the tax.

Joan follows the steps set out above to work out her tax for the 2009/10 tax year:

Step 1: She writes down all her income in three columns, remembering to use the gross amount of her building society interest, and adds it up:

A	B	C
State Pension £5,257.20 Pension from job £2,640.00 **Total A = £7,897.20**	Interest on savings grossed up **Total B = £1,500**	She gets no dividends on shares so **Total C = £0.00**

Step 2: Joan answers 'No'. She didn't make any Gift Aid donations or pension contributions. As Joan is over 75, she is entitled to the highest

level of personal allowance. As her total income is less than £22,900, she can claim the full higher allowance of £9,640 for someone over 75.

She skips the steps about dividends – even if she had some the basic rate tax has already been paid – and goes straight to Step 8.

Step 8: She adds her income up. It comes to £9,397.20. That is less than her personal allowance of £9,640 so she answers 'No'. She has no Tax (D) so she goes to Step 11 with the knowledge that she has no tax to pay.

Step 11: Joan has no tax to pay. But she had £300 deducted automatically from her building society interest. She checks back and finds that interest has been deducted every year. Last year, some tax was due but only at 10%. In earlier years tax was also due, but again much of it at 10%. She claims back the overpaid tax on Form R40, and to make sure, she looks up the figures and claims it back for each year back to 2003/04. She sends them off and gets a nice cheque for more than £600. She fills in form R85 so that in future her interest is paid gross.

Tax-saving tip: *With falling interest rates and rising tax allowances, many people over 65 who paid tax in the past do not have to pay it this year. Many people have tax deducted from their savings interest who should not pay tax or only pay it at the 10% rate – which still exists for savings interest in some*

circumstances. If you are not liable to pay tax, make sure you do not have tax deducted from interest on your savings in a bank or building society account by signing Form R85 and claiming tax back for previous years. If your income is within £2,440 of your personal allowance then you may be able to get some tax back.

2. Married couple

Ravi is 75 and married to **Sangeeta**, who is 63. They both pay tax and must work out their tax separately.

Ravi: He has retired and receives a State Pension of £117.10 a week, which includes some SERPS (officially called Additional Pension) from a previous job. He also receives an occupational pension from his last employer of £600 a month gross. He and Sangeeta have a joint building society account on which they receive net interest of £504 in the year. The Revenue will treat this as being split equally between them – £252 each. That is grossed up as £252 x 5 ÷ 4 = £315.

Step 1: Ravi writes down his income for 2009/10:

A	B	C
State Pension £6,089.20 Pension from job £7,200.00 **Total A = £13,289.20**	Half interest on savings grossed up **Total B = £315.00**	He gets no dividends on shares so **Total C = £0.00**

Step 2: Ravi was born in July 1934. So he answers 'No'. He adds up his income. He has no Gift Aid or pension to deduct and his total income is well below £22,900, so he looks up his personal allowance for someone aged 75 or more and he gets the full amount of £9,640. He is not blind.

He skips the steps about dividends and higher rate tax and goes straight to Step 8.

Step 8: His income A plus B is bigger than his allowance P. So he goes to Step 9.

Step 9: He has come from Step 8 so he adds his income up and subtracts his allowance.

A =	£13,289.20
B =	£ 315.00
	£13,1604.20
His personal allowance P is	£ 9,640.00
He subtracts it	£ 3,964.20

He multiplies the answer by 0.2 which gives £792.84. He writes that down and calls it 'Z'.

Is A + B bigger than P? It is, so he answers 'Yes'.

He renames Z 'Tax (B)' and goes to Step 10.

Step 10: Ravi has one amount of tax due from Step 9 – Tax (B) which is £792.84. He calls it 'Y'.

Ravi was 75 in July 2009, so he was born before 6 April 1935, and can get the Married Couple's Allowance, which is £6,965. He doesn't give any of it to his wife and his income is well below £29,230 so he needn't reduce it. 10% of £6,965 is £696.50 which he calls 'M'.

Is Y bigger than M?

Yes. So he takes M from Y. £792.84 – £696.50 = £96.34. That amount is the tax he should have paid.

He goes to Step 11.

Step 11: He has already paid his share of the tax on his building society account, which amounts to 20% of half the grossed-up interest, which is £63. So he should have tax of £96.34 – £63 = £33.34 deducted from his pension, at the rate of £2.78 a month. When he checks, he finds that he has had more than this deducted. He does not know why – nor does the Revenue – but he claims a refund.

Sangeeta then does her tax. She has recently retired from full-time work but does not get a pension from her former employer. She gets the married woman's pension of £57.05 a week, paid as a result of Ravi's contributions. She still works three mornings a week and her 12 hours at £6 an hour come to £72 a week. And she has her share of the interest on their joint savings – £315 gross.

Step 1: She adds up her income:

A	B	C
State Pension £57.05 x 52 £2,966.60 Earnings £72 x 52 £3,744.00 **Total A = £6,710.60**	Half interest on savings grossed up **Total B = £315.00**	She gets no dividends on shares so **Total C = £0.00**

Step 2: Sangeeta is 63 so she answers 'Yes' and is entitled to the basic personal allowance of £6,475. She is not blind.

Step 3: She has no dividends. So she breathes a sigh of relief and skips to Step 6.

Step 6: She adds A and B, which is £7,025.60. She adds her personal allowance to £37,400 which comes to £43,875. That is more than A + B so she answers 'No' and goes to Step 8.

Step 8: Total A + Total B is more than her personal tax allowance so she answers 'Yes' and goes to Step 9.

Step 9: She adds A and B and subtracts P. £6,710.60 + £315 – £6,475 = £550.60. She multiplies that by 0.2 which is £110.12. She calls that 'Z'.

She adds P to £2,440 which is £6,475 + £2,440 = £8,915.

A is not bigger than this, so she answers 'No' – and enters the weird world of Step 9a!

Step 9a: Is her income A bigger than her personal allowance P?

- **Yes:** So she moves on to the next question: Is Z bigger than £488? It isn't.
- **No:** So she multiplies B by 0.1: £315 x 0.1 = £31.50. She subtracts it from Z: £110.12 – £31.50 = £78.62. She calls that Tax (B).

That wasn't as hard as she thought. She goes to Step 10.

Step 10: She is not entitled to a Married Couple's Allowance – Ravi has that and she does not want any of it transferred to her.

She goes to Step 11.

Step 11: She checks her wages and finds that over the year she has paid £44.60 in tax. She has also had tax at 20% deducted automatically from her interest. Her share of that is £63. Altogether she has paid £44.60 + £63 = £107.60 which is £28.98 more than the tax due she has worked out. So she calls the tax back helpline and they send her the forms to claim £28.98 back from the Revenue. She also claims for up to six previous years and is delighted to find that she also gets some money back from those years as well.

Tax-saving tip: *If you are only due to pay tax at 10% on your savings, then you can claim back half the tax the bank or building society has deducted from your interest.*

3. Couple where one partner pays no tax

Sid is 69 and his wife **Lillian** is 67. In 2009/10 Sid receives the State Pension, which in his case is £102.50 a week, and a pension from his job of £1,450 a month. Sid also put a lump sum in the building society in his name when he retired and despite falling interest rates should provide £1,300 in 2009/10, which he and Lillian found very useful. Sid grosses it up, which means he counts £1,625 as his income.

Lillian gets the married woman's pension of £57.05 a week on Sid's contributions but she does get a bit extra amounting to £3.12 a week – a total of £3,128.84 a year. This is much less than her personal allowance of £9,490, so she should pay no tax. Sid, however, pays quite a lot.

Step 1: Sid writes down his income.

A	B	C
State Pension £102.50 x 52 £5,330 Works pension £1,450 x 12 £17,400 **Total A = £22,730**	Interest grossed up **Total B = £1,625**	He gets no dividends on shares so **Total C = £0.00**

Step 2: He was born before 6 April 1945.

He makes no pension contributions but he does give £20 each Christmas to the church and registers it for Gift Aid. He grosses that up by dividing by 4 and multiplying by 5 which comes to £25. So his total income is £22,730 + £1,625 – £25 = £24,330.

He looks up the personal allowance for someone aged 69 and it is £9,490. But Sid's total income of £24,330 is more than the income limit of £22,900 for the higher levels of personal allowance. He takes one from the other and gets £1,430 so he halves that (see page 37) and deducts the £715 from his maximum personal allowance of £9,490 to get £8,775, which is his personal allowance for 2009/10.

His allowance is still more than the minimum so he does not need to worry about dividends or whether he pays higher rate tax. He goes straight to Step 8.

Step 8: Sid adds up A and B and it is a lot bigger than his personal allowance P. So he goes to Step 9.

Step 9: He has already added A and B so he deducts P: £24,330 – £8,775 = £15,555. He multiplies it by 0.2 to give £3,111. That is Z.

Is A bigger than P + £2,440?

Sid sees that it is and answers 'Yes'. He renames Z 'Tax (B)' and goes to Step 10.

Step 10: Neither Sid nor Lillian were born before 6 April 1935, so Sid cannot get the Married Couple's Allowance. He goes to Step 11.

Step 11: Sid checks his tax and finds he has paid tax on his savings through the automatic deduction by the building society. Tax on his State Pension and his occupational pension was deducted through PAYE from his occupational pension. For some reason, it is not quite right.

Sid tells the tax office but is advised that he could actually pay less tax if he transferred the money in his building society account to Lillian. If he had done so before the start of the tax year, Lillian's income this tax year would then have consisted of the State Pension of £3,128.84 plus the interest of £1,625. This total of £4,753.84 would still be well below her personal allowance of £9,490 and so no tax would be due on it. As a non-taxpayer she could have applied to have the interest paid gross without the tax being deducted. That would have saved Sid the £325 tax due on the interest.

But the savings don't stop there. Sid's total income would then have been £22,730, which is below the £22,900 limit for the age allowance. So he would get the full higher personal allowance of £9,490. That would have cut his tax bill by a further £143, so altogether he could have saved £468, which is more than £9 a week. Sid makes the change at once and, although the savings are not quite so great this year, they have a holiday on the proceeds. Next year they will save the full amount.

 Tax-saving tip: *If one partner pays no tax or tax at a lower rate, you can save tax by transferring income or savings to that partner. This is especially helpful if it brings down the taxpaying partner's income enough to get the full age allowance.*

Remember that although transferring assets can save tax, there can also be disadvantages. For example, if Lillian had to go into a care home after Sid transferred all the savings into her name, those savings would mean she would get no help with her fees. If you do transfer assets, this must be a genuine gift, so the recipient has complete control over the asset – you must not keep an interest in it yourself.

Conclusion

Phew! Well done for getting to the end of the chapter.

Always remember two things. First, the Revenue makes a lot of mistakes. So always check what it tells you. If you come up with a different answer or you just do not understand something, don't be embarrassed to ask the Revenue to explain its calculations. Second, the rules about paying tax are very biased in favour of the Revenue. If you make a mistake or miss a payment, you can be penalised or fined. If the Revenue makes a mistake or misses a deadline, the closest you get to an apology will usually be a shrug. So err on the side of caution and claim any overpaid tax back later.

Self-employment

It is easy to become self-employed in retirement without realising it. For example, you may in fact be self-employed if you:

- buy things to sell at car boot sales or on eBay;
- write the odd article for money;
- become a local handyman for neighbours who pay you; or
- do regular babysitting for money.

There is no minimum amount of earnings before you become self-employed. Strictly speaking, if you do any work or trading for money on your own account, you are self-employed. And although your earnings may be too low to pay tax or National Insurance, you still count as self-employed.

If you are self-employed, you will have to fill in a self-assessment form, work out your own profits and pay your own Income Tax. If your turnover is less than £15,000 the details required on the form are very few.

If you are under State Pension age, you may also have to pay your own National Insurance contributions (NICs: see pages 53–56).

If your annual turnover is more than £67,000, you may also have to charge Value Added Tax (VAT) on your invoices and pay that to the Revenue.

If your turnover is less than £150,000, you may benefit from the flat-rate VAT scheme (see page 86).

Income from self-employment is added to income from pensions and other sources to determine the total amount of tax you are liable to pay. You will have income from self-employment if you are in business on your own account, even on a part-time or occasional basis, provided that the money you earn exceeds your business expenses.

The Revenue has pages about working for yourself at www.hmrc.gov.uk/leaflets/se1.htm *or you can download the leaflet at* www.hmrc.gov.uk/leaflets/se1.pdf. *You can also find out more from The No-nonsense Guide to Government Rules and Regulations for Setting up your Business, which is also published by the government. You can read it at the website* www.tinyurl.com/a778q *or get a copy by calling 0845 600 9 006.*

Notifying the Revenue

If you become self-employed, you are legally obliged to notify the Revenue when you start. Registration is required for both Income Tax and National Insurance and you can register for both at the same time. If you don't register within the first three full months of self-employment, you may be liable for a penalty of £100. If you have still not registered by 6 October following the end of the tax year in which you started up, further penalties may be due. You must register even if you earn very little, or nothing at all, from your self-employment.

You can notify the Revenue that you are self-employed simply by writing to your local tax office. Always keep a copy of any letter you send. A better method may be to obtain leaflet SE1 and fill in form CWF1, which it contains. You can also register by phone – call the Revenue helpline for the newly self-employed on 08459 15 45 15.

Your accounting date

Once the Revenue knows you are self-employed, you should be sent a self-assessment form each April, including the pages for self-employment. If your turnover is less than £15,000, you will normally be sent the Short Tax Return, which is easier to fill in. On this you must declare your business income and expenses. The balance of your income, less your expenses, is your taxable profit – in other words, it is the income on which you are liable to pay tax.

Although the Income Tax year runs from 6 April to the following 5 April, you can fix your own 'accounting year' over which you work out your income and expenses and arrive at your profit or loss. For any tax year, your tax calculation will be based on your profit for the 12 months up to your accounting date which ends in that tax year.

When you start in self-employment it can be worthwhile to fix your accounting year to end on 30 April. This year, for example, that would mean that the profit from the year 1 May 2008 to 30 April 2009 is taxed in the tax year 2009/10. If your accounting year runs from 1 April 2008 to

31 March 2009 (just a month earlier), that income would be taxed a whole year earlier in 2008/09. So by fixing your accounting year to end on 30 April, you in effect put off the tax you pay by almost a year. It also means that you know the exact figures when you come to fill in your tax return.

When a business starts and ends

Special rules apply in the first two years of a new business and when a business ends. For the first year, you are taxed on your profit from the date you start until the following 5 April. For the second year, you are taxed on your profit for the 12 months up to your accounting date in that tax year, provided that the date is at least a year after your business started – if it is not, you are taxed on your profit for the first 12 months of business.

These rules may mean that some part of your profit is taken into account in calculating your taxable profit for more than one tax year. If so, you are entitled to 'overlap relief' when your business ends – the effect being that, over the lifetime of your business, you are taxed on no more and no less than the full amount of your profit. It can get very complicated and it is worth consulting an accountant or tax adviser, at least in the first and last years of your business.

Tax-saving tip: *Choose your accounting date to reduce the tax you pay. When your business starts and ends, get the tax you pay checked carefully by an accountant or tax adviser.*

Business expenses

There is normally no difficulty in deciding how much your business income is, but working out your expenses may be more difficult. The situation is fairly clear-cut if, for example, you are buying goods to resell; but determining other expenses is less straightforward – particularly when expenses are partly for business purposes and partly private.

For example, if you work from home you need a phone. Unless you go to the expense of having a separate business line, your calls will be a mixture of business and personal. The cost of business calls and a share of the phone rental can be deducted from your turnover. To work out the business share, get an itemised bill, which BT and many other phone companies provide at no cost. You can then see the proportion of the costs that are business. There is no need to count them up each time; do it once and then in future you can charge that proportion of your bill to the business. Keep the evidence in case the Revenue queries it. It is sensible to monitor the position from time to time, especially if the business grows.

You can also charge a proportion of the cost of running your car – including petrol, car tax, breakdown service, insurance, and any interest on a loan to buy it. Keep a note of business and personal mileage to work out the business share.

If you work from home, you will also be able to claim a proportion of domestic expenses. But there are no clear rules about what expenses you can charge or how you work out a fair proportion.

You should be able to charge a proportion of gas, electricity, insurance of the contents that are relevant to your business, rent, mortgage interest (but not capital repayments), and Council Tax as business expenses. You may also be able to charge the cost of water if you have a water meter but not otherwise.

The normal way to work out the proportion is to count the main rooms in the house, excluding the bathroom. Some tax inspectors might let you ignore the kitchen too; others may try to count the bathroom. If there are four main rooms and you mainly work from one of them and use that room for little else, then you can charge a quarter of the costs to the business. Alternatively you can measure the floor area of your home and of your office and use that proportion. Whatever method you use, pick one that you think is fair and stick by it.

Tax-saving tip: *Whenever you buy anything for your business (even a newspaper or magazine), or you spend anything on travel (even a bus fare), get a receipt and keep it.*

Capital allowances

Until 2007/08 there were complex rules about how you claimed for the cost of capital items such as a computer or your car. From 2008/09 a much simpler system applies to everything except vehicles. You simply charge 100% of the capital cost of the item bought for your business in the year you buy it, up to a maximum of £50,000 for the year. So if you buy a computer for £750 in 2009/10 you can charge £750 as a business expense that year. If you spend more than £50,000 you get a first year allowance of 40% of the extra amount you spend.

This new Annual Investment Allowance and the 40% first year allowance do not apply to vehicles. So if you charge a share of your car to the business and you buy a new one you will only be able to charge 20% of the business share in the first year. So if the car costs £7,000 and you allocate half its use to your business, that is £3,500, and you can then charge 20% of that which is £700. The next year you can charge 20% of the remaining value so deduct £700 from £3,500 and work out 20% of that, which is £560, and so on.

The Revenue Self-assessment Help Sheet HS222 gives information about business expenses and capital allowances. You can get a copy from the Revenue Orderline on 08459 000 404 or from the website at www.hmrc.gov.uk/helpsheets/hs222.pdf.

Keeping records

On your tax return, you are simply expected to declare your income and expenses. The Revenue does not normally expect to see invoices, receipts or other original records. Nor does it expect to be sent accounts prepared by an accountant. But you must keep proper records of all these things so that you can work out your income and expenditure. You must also keep all your bank or building society statements or passbooks.

It is essential that you have an accounts book, and write it up regularly. If you keep records on your computer, always back up the files and print them out regularly. If you have an internet bank or savings account, print out your statements each month and keep them in a file. Remember to order and keep an annual statement of any interest on savings.

If you are self-employed or rent out property, you are legally obliged to keep all records relating to a particular tax year for a minimum of five years from the date you filed your return for that year. You can now destroy records for the tax year 2002/03. The tax return for the following year, 2003/04, was due in to the Revenue by 31 January 2005. Five years from then is 31 January 2010. So you could destroy your self-employment records for the tax year 2003/04 on 1 February 2010. But if the Revenue has embarked on an enquiry into your tax affairs, you have to keep the relevant records until that enquiry is finished. These dates have not changed with the changed filing dates for paper forms.

For more information, see the Revenue leaflet SABK4 Self-assessment: A general guide to keeping records, which was available online at www.hmrc.gov.uk/pdfs/sabk4.pdf, *though this leaflet may be altered in 2009/10.*

When tax is paid

Tax on income from self-employment is normally paid in two instalments and a balancing payment. For the 2009/10 tax year, the first instalment will be due on 31 January 2010 and the second on 31 July 2010. If it turns out you have paid too little tax, then a balancing payment will become due on 31 January 2011.

The amount of tax payable under the first two instalments is based upon the amount of tax you were liable to pay for the previous year. Half that amount will normally be due in each instalment. If, however, you believe that your tax will be less than that for the previous year, you can apply to your tax office to have the instalments reduced.

If the total tax due is less than £1,000, no instalment payments will be required and you pay all of it on 31 January 2010. If you don't pay the correct amount of tax on the proper date, you will be liable to pay interest on unpaid tax.

Value Added Tax

If you are self-employed or run a small business, you will have to register for VAT if your turnover – which is the total income of your business, not the profit – exceeds £68,000. Once registered, you must charge VAT at the standard rate (normally 17.5% but reduced to 15% from 1 December 2008 to 31 December 2009) on goods or services you supply. Some items are exempt from VAT or zero-rated and you do not have to charge VAT on those, and a very few are liable at 5%.

The VAT you collect from customers has to be passed on to the Revenue. But you can reclaim the VAT you pay on goods or services you buy. Each quarter (or annually if your turnover is low and you prefer to do it that way) you submit a VAT return showing the amount of VAT collected from your customers and the amount you are reclaiming on goods or services you have bought. You take one from the other and pay the difference – or make a claim for a refund if you have paid more VAT than you have collected. The Revenue is encouraging everyone to file their forms and pay online and soon that will be compulsory, so you might as well start now.

Money-saving tip: *In some circumstances, even if your gross business income does not exceed the £68,000 limit, it may be a good idea to register for VAT. If you register you can recover the VAT on goods or services you buy for business purposes. So get a VAT receipt for everything bought for your business. But registering for VAT will involve you in more paperwork and accounting. So think carefully before doing it.*

Flat-rate scheme

If your taxable turnover excluding VAT is £150,000 or less, you may want to pay your VAT under the flat-rate scheme. Instead of all the fiddly working out of VAT charged and paid, you can pay a flat-rate percentage of your turnover. The percentages range from 4% to 13.5% of your turnover including VAT but are lower for the period when VAT is cut to 15%. The exact rate depends on the type of business you run. These rates are reduced by 1% in your first year of trading. The savings can be considerable for some businesses. You can stay in the scheme until your turnover, including VAT, reaches £225,000 in the year – check that limit on each anniversary of joining the scheme.

Tax-saving tip: *The flat-rate scheme can bring big savings to some businesses. Consider it if your turnover excluding VAT is between £68,000 and £150,000 a year.*

A detailed booklet on the flat-rate scheme called Notice 733 is available from the Revenue or go to its website www.hmrc.gov.uk and search for 'Notice 733 Flat Rate Scheme'.

For further information on VAT, contact the VAT National Advice Service on 0845 010 9000.

Capital Gains Tax

You may have to pay some Capital Gains Tax (CGT) if you sell or give away an asset that has increased in value since you bought it. An 'asset' is something you own, such as shares, antiques or property. It is not money as such – although in rare circumstances foreign currency may count as an asset. The profit on which you are taxed is called a capital gain.

Major changes in Capital Gains Tax began on 6 April 2008. The changes make CGT much simpler. But the main purpose of the change was to raise more money, so it will mean an increase in CGT in many cases. The new rules apply to any disposal of an item on 6 April 2008 or later. If you disposed of something before that date the old rules will apply and you should seek advice about what tax you should have paid.

Not all gains are taxed. Some items are free of CGT:

- your only or main private residence (see pages 90–92);
- private cars;
- National Savings certificates;

- most British government stocks, usually called 'gilts';
- personal belongings worth up to £6,000;
- Individual Savings Accounts (ISAs);
- proceeds of most life insurance policies;
- Premium Bond prizes, betting winnings, National Lottery winnings; and
- gifts to registered charities.

CGT applies to people who normally live in the UK and consider the UK their home, no matter where in the world their property is located.

Two further exemptions limit the amount that any individual pays in CGT:

- **Any gift you make to a husband, wife or civil partner with whom you live is entirely free of CGT.** But if they then dispose of the asset, tax is due and will be calculated on the value from the date on which you – not they – acquired it.
- **In the tax year 2009/10 you can have up to £10,100 of capital gains without paying tax.** Husbands, wives and civil partners are taxed independently on any gains, and each partner is entitled to a separate exempt amount of £10,100.

Anything above the limit is charged at a flat rate of 18%.

Certain expenses can also be deducted. You can deduct the costs of acquiring or disposing of the asset, such as fees to a broker or taxes. You can also deduct the costs of improving the asset – such as having a picture professionally restored or by adding an extension to a let property. Your total capital gains in a year can be reduced if you have made capital losses on other things – for example, if you sell shares for less than you paid for them.

Losses can be carried forward from one year to the next. If your overall net gain is £10,100 or less, there will be no CGT to pay. But you must set any loss against gains you have made in the same tax year, even if the gains are covered by your annual exemption. A loss made on an asset that is exempt from CGT cannot be claimed.

 Tax-saving tip: *If you make a CGT loss, tell the Revenue – otherwise you may not be able to carry it forward.*

Before April 2008, assets bought on 6 April 1998 or later had the gain reduced or tapered. The gain on assets bought before 6 April 1998 could also be reduced by a process called 'indexation'. Taper relief and indexation were scrapped from April 2008. Complex rules governing the way capital gains were calculated for items acquired before 31 March 1982 were also abolished.

Your home

Capital Gains Tax is not normally charged when you sell or give away the home you live in, as long as:

- it has been your 'main' residence throughout your ownership (even if this condition is not met, you may be entitled to some relief); and
- the grounds do not exceed half a hectare (which is a bit more than one acre). That rule is waived if the grounds are provided for the reasonable

enjoyment of the property. That is a very subjective test, so if the Revenue tries to apply CGT to a large garden, appeal.

If you own and live in two properties, you can nominate one of them to be your 'main' residence as long as you have lived in it at some point. You need to do this within two years of acquiring the second property.

If you do have a second property, then the last three years of ownership are exempt from CGT whatever you have used it for, as long as it has been your home at some point. If the other property has been occupied by a dependent relative rent free since before 6 April 1988, it may be exempt from CGT. A couple who are married or civil partners can have only one 'main residence' between them. Other couples can have one each.

Tax saving tip: *If you are an unmarried couple and have two properties, register one each as your main residence. That will avoid CGT when you sell either of them.*

If you separate from your partner or spouse and one of you moves out of the jointly owned home, CGT can arise when the home is sold. It will have to be paid by the partner who has moved out, as the home is no longer their main residence. As long as it is sold within three years of the partner moving out, no CGT will be due. After that, some CGT may be due, but the calculation is very complex and you should seek advice.

More information is available from the Low Incomes Tax Reform Group website at www.litrg.org.uk/help/pensioners/ incomesover/life_events_separation.cfm.

If you have a lodger in the home you live in as your main residence who shares a kitchen and bathroom and living space with you and who lives as a member of the family, you should not have to pay CGT when you sell the property.

But if you let part of your home to someone who does not live as a member of your family, CGT may be payable. That applies even if the rent is exempt from Income Tax under the rent-a-room scheme (see page 4). The gain on which CGT will be calculated is related to the proportion of the property that is rented and the period of letting compared to the total period of ownership. But a certain amount of the gain will normally be exempt, so you may not have to pay any CGT. Ask at your tax office if you need further details.

If you use part of your home exclusively for business purposes, then a proportion of the property may be liable to CGT when you sell it.

Tax-saving tip: *If you use a room to run a small business or for self-employment, make sure you use it for something else as well, even if only occasionally. That stops the Revenue saying it is used 'exclusively' for business.*

Selling shares

Shares, unit trust units and shares in OEICs (see pages 32–33) give rise to capital gains or losses when you sell them or give them away. But when you sell or give away shares of the same type, in the same company, that you acquired at different times, there are special rules that govern the way gains and losses are worked out. This doesn't apply to shares or unit trusts held as part of an ISA, which are exempt from tax, nor to shares given to charity under the Gift Aid scheme.

If you give shares to someone who is not your spouse or civil partner, then the difference between the price you paid and their current market value is treated as a capital gain. You may be able to deduct some expenses. But if after that the amount exceeds your annual exemption, then you will be liable for CGT.

Shares in a company you worked for that you acquired tax free under the Save As You Earn scheme may be liable to CGT but there are usually ways to avoid it. Consult your employer.

Windfalls

If you are a member of a building society or a mutual insurance company which changes its status to become a company, then you may well be paid a windfall. That payment is made to compensate you for the value of your membership. The Revenue assumes that you got it for nothing and so the whole amount of the windfall can be counted as a capital gain. If it is big enough, CGT can be due on it. Often, the organisations making these payments will introduce some special device to reduce or avoid this tax. But always check if you get one.

For more information on CGT see the Revenue website www.hmrc.gov.uk/cgt, *where you can download more detailed guides.*

Inheritance Tax

Inheritance Tax (IHT) is probably the most hated of the taxes in this book – which is strange because (a) when it is due you are dead; (b) someone else pays it; and (c) the vast majority of people die with too little money and possessions for any IHT to be due.

People fear – and hate – IHT because of the rise in price of their homes in the last decade or so. Despite recent falls in property prices, many people still own a property that is worth enough by itself to mean the tax would be due if they died now. But big changes announced in October 2007 mean that a home owned by a married couple or civil partners is much less likely to exceed the Inheritance Tax threshold. The new rules were announced on 9 October 2007 and began from that date.

How IHT is calculated

IHT is one of the simpler taxes. In most cases it's quite easy to see if your heirs would have any IHT to pay if you died tomorrow:

- Add up the value of everything you own, including your house, any investments, savings, personal property, and any payments your heirs will get from life insurance policies which are not written in trust. Your estate includes all your assets, wherever in the world these are located.

- Add to that any substantial gifts you have made in the past seven years, but do not include any gifts covered by the exemptions listed on pages 97–99.

- Take away any money owed on a mortgage. If you have raised money on your home, then only count the value of your home minus any debt on it.

- Take away any other debts. When you die, unpaid bills, taxes and funeral expenses will be deducted from your estate before it is passed to your heirs.

- Take away from the total anything you intend to leave to your spouse or civil partner, or to charity.

- If you are in business or farming, there may be further amounts to deduct from the value of the business.

If the final amount is less than the threshold for IHT – currently £325,000 – no tax will be due.

In 2009/10 the threshold is £325,000. The government has already announced that it will increase to £350,000 for 2010/11. But when a widowed person dies they may now have a threshold up to twice those amounts (see pages 100–102).

If your total is more than this, it is likely that some IHT will be due. It is charged at a single rate of 40% on the excess over the threshold.

- So a single person's estate of £425,000 will be taxed at 40% of £100,000 – which is £40,000.

No IHT is due on anything left to your wife or husband or civil partner as long as you both normally live in the UK. Under the new rules which began in October 2007 leaving everything to your spouse is normally the best course.

Ways of reducing IHT

The best way to reduce the IHT that has to be paid is to spend your money now. That way you get to use it and the taxman gets less – and of course so do your heirs. Fortunately (for them) there are other ways of reducing the tax due.

Gifts made more than seven years before your death are completely exempt from IHT. So if you give money away and live another seven years then no IHT will be due on that amount. If you give away more than £325,000 (or whatever the threshold is when you die) before your death, then the tax is reduced on the gift if you die more than three years after making it.

Other gifts are also not counted even if you do die within seven years of making them, including:

- Gifts to your husband, wife or civil partner.
- Small gifts of up to £250 each to any number of people.
- Regular gifts out of income that do not reduce your standard of living.
- Wedding gifts of up to £5,000 to your child, or £2,500 to your grandchild or great-grandchild, or £1,000 to anyone else.

> *When **Monica's** husband Stan died she got a considerable pension from his old job. Now he has gone she goes out far less and finds that she never spends her monthly income. Her current account balance rises by about £250 each month. When her granddaughter Jody goes to university, she decides to give her a regular £200 a month. She writes a letter and keeps it with her will saying that this is money from her income and does not reduce her standard of living.*

- Gifts to a registered charity, a national museum or art gallery, a university or a political party.
- Gifts to a child of yours (but not a grandchild) while they are in full-time education if the money is given for their maintenance or the costs of their education or training.
- Other gifts totalling no more than £3,000 in a year. You can also carry this allowance forward from the previous year, so that it can be worth £6,000 if you gave nothing the previous year.

These reliefs and exemptions are personal. So a husband and wife – or two civil partners – can each give these amounts.

Tax-saving tip: *If they have made no gifts to reduce IHT in the previous year, a couple can give away £12,000 between them in one tax year without it counting for IHT. Even if all the assets are owned*

> *by one of them, that person can give £6,000 to their spouse or civil partner, which will be exempt, and then each can give £6,000 to a child.*

Don't give your children or other heirs money that you will need yourself.

Also beware of giving away shares or anything that may have grown in value. If you do, then Capital Gains Tax may be payable on the gain as if you had sold it at market value. It is safer to give away cash.

Some charities try to get you to leave them money in your will as a way of 'tax planning' because the gifts you make are free of Inheritance Tax. Leaving money to charity may be a good thing. But it's not sensible tax planning. Your heirs will in effect be the ones who make the gift.

> **Jane** *dies with an estate of £425,000. She decided to leave £100,000 to charity, so her estate is £325,000 and no IHT is due. Her two children share her £325,000 estate and get £162,500 each.*
>
> *Her neighbour* **Ken** *dies with an identical estate of £425,000. He made no legacies to charity. His estate is £100,000 above the IHT threshold, so there is £40,000 of tax to pay – leaving a net £385,000 for his two children to share. They get £192,500 each, which is an extra £30,000 each.*

So the heirs do better if you make no legacies to charity. That is simply because 60% of something is better than 100% of nothing. Please leave money to charity. But don't call it tax planning. It isn't.

Your home

For the vast majority of people, it is the value of their home which takes their estate into Inheritance Tax territory. Until recently, couples were advised to take complicated steps to reduce the tax due so that each left something to their children.

But rules announced by the Chancellor on 9 October 2007 changed that advice completely. Now it is normally best to leave everything to your spouse or civil partner.

A widow or widower, or bereaved civil partner, who dies from 9 October 2007 gets their own allowance of £325,000 and their heirs can also add on the unused allowance of the widowed person's late spouse. That means many widows or widowers who die this year will, in effect, have an allowance of £650,000 rather than the £325,000 allowed to single people.

£ If the first spouse to die leaves nothing to anyone else, then the surviving spouse has an allowance of double the current allowance on their death.

£ If the first to die has left money or property to other people, then the allowance that can be passed on is reduced.

The calculation is done like this:

£ The amount they left to people other than their spouse is worked out as a proportion of the allowance that was current at the time. For example, if the first spouse died in 2004/05 when the allowance was £263,000 and they left £50,000 directly to their children, they have used up 50 ÷ 263 or 19% of their allowance. That leaves 81% to be passed on to the survivor.

£ When the surviving spouse dies they get their own allowance plus the unused percentage times the current allowance. So if the second spouse dies this tax year they will get £325,000 as their own allowance and £325,000 x 81% = £263,250 as their inherited allowance, making a total of £588,250. No tax will be due on that amount. Inheritance Tax will be due on anything they leave above that amount of £588,250.

£ If the first to die leaves property or money to other people which uses up the whole of their allowance then there will be no allowance to pass on to the survivor.

The couple must be married or civil partners at the time of the first death. If they have divorced before that then no allowance can be passed on. A widow or widower who remarries and is then bereaved again can inherit an allowance from both late spouses, but the total inherited allowance cannot be more than 100% of the allowance at the time of the widow or widower's death.

The October 2007 rule completely turns on its head advice previously given to couples. To make the most of this rule people should leave everything to their spouse. If they want money, property or valuables to go to their heirs they should not state that in their will. Instead they should tell their spouse what they would like (and it is safer not to do this in writing) and let the survivor make those gifts later so that they count as lifetime gifts and the rules described earlier apply. Part of the value may be within one of the tax-free, lifetime gifts and if the spouse survives seven years after the gifts are made then no tax will be due. When the second spouse dies, the threshold for IHT will be higher and the estate will get that higher allowance in full twice.

Couples who have already written wills to leave some of their property to children or other heirs should consider rewriting them to leave everything to each other. If they have left property in trust they should seek advice about whether those trust provisions are now necessary or effective. Even after a death a will can usually be rewritten for up to two years if all the heirs agree.

Peter and **Judy** *own their family home – which today is worth £575,000 – and Peter had £75,000 in savings but not much else. In May 2005, Peter died. He left the house to Judy but they had agreed he should divide the cash between their two children. As the cash was well below the allowance – then £275,000 – no IHT was due. In January 2010 Judy also dies, leaving the house and her possessions – total £585,000 – to the children.*

Peter used up £75,000 or 27% of his £275,000 allowance, leaving 72.7% for Judy to take over. In 2009/10 the IHT allowance is £325,000. When Judy dies, her estate will get that allowance plus another 72.7% of it, totalling £561,364. Her estate exceeds this by £23,636 so tax is due at 40% on that, which is £9,454.55.

But if Peter had left everything to Judy and she then gave the maximum exempt amount of £3,000 a year between her children – a total of £12,000 – she would have died with an estate of £648,000. There would have been two allowances due in full, worth £650,000. So no tax would have been due, saving her children £9,455.

If a widow was widowed many years ago, the evidence for what was left in the estate may have disappeared. In that case, it is sensible for the widow to set down their recollection of it in writing and keep that with their will. This can help avoid conflict with the Revenue when they die.

The rules are more complicated for people who were widowed before 13 March 1975. Although the principle is the same, their initial tax was calculated under estate duty rules and there may be little or no allowance to inherit even if everything was left to them.

If a widow or widower remarries and already has 100% of their late spouse's allowance to inherit, then it may be worth splitting the estate so that each leaves half to their heirs. If you are in this position, seek advice.

Don't try to avoid Inheritance Tax by giving away something but continuing to benefit from it. For example, if you give away your home but continue to live in it, the value of your home will still count as part of your estate even if the legal title actually belongs to someone else – such as one of your children.

If you live with someone to whom you are not married (and you are not civil partners), there is no IHT exemption on gifts or inheritance between you. So if your home is worth more than the IHT threshold of £325,000 and the one who owns the house dies, the surviving partner can face a big IHT bill just to remain in the home.

The Revenue will let you pay the tax due on a property in 10 annual instalments but interest will be charged. That can also happen if you own half each and the property is worth more than twice the IHT threshold. There is little you can do about this danger, but you should be aware of it.

In Scotland a new status of 'cohabitant' has been created, but although this gives unmarried couples some rights to each other's property on separation or death, it does not help with Inheritance Tax.

Falling property prices

The value of property is now falling and by the time the estate is finalised the value of property that was inherited can be less than it was at the time of death. Strictly speaking, tax is due on the value of the estate on the day of the death. But the Revenue may be sympathetic if the value has fallen considerably since the date of death.

If the property is sold on the open market within four years of the death and realises less than the amount used to work out Inheritance Tax, the Revenue has to recalculate the tax using the new value. A similar rule applies to shares but they must be sold within one year of the death. The claim for this reduction can be made up to six years after the tax was paid.

Other ways to avoid the tax

If you have a life insurance policy that pays out on your death, make sure that the policy is 'written in trust'. This means that the proceeds do not go directly to your dependants. Instead they are paid into a trust, which then passes them on to your dependants – that avoids the proceeds counting as part of your estate. But if the value of the policy is more than £325,000, then some tax may be due.

If your policy is worth more than £325,000, consult your insurer or an accountant.

Trusts can be a way to avoid IHT, but they can be expensive to set up and run, and are mainly suitable for people with estates worth considerably more than the IHT limit of £325,000. New restrictions mean they are less useful than they were in the past and the government may restrict their use again.

Some insurance companies and financial consultants sell plans to reduce or avoid Inheritance Tax. Such schemes can be complicated – juggling the ownership of money or making gifts into or from trusts – and frequently involve taking out an insurance policy. These

105

schemes are often designed to generate commission for the salesperson rather than benefit you. The government has taken action to stop some of these schemes working, and it has warned that it will take action against any scheme that achieves nothing but the reduction of tax. Before committing yourself to any scheme, be sure it has the approval of the Revenue, and discuss it with an impartial professional adviser such as a solicitor or an accountant. Such schemes are best avoided.

For more information, see the Revenue website http://www.hmrc.gov.uk/ inheritancetax. *You can contact the Probate and IHT Helpline on 0845 30 20 900.*

Stamp Duty Land Tax

One of the latest wheezes to part us from our money is Stamp Duty Land Tax. When it was just known as 'stamp duty' it was paid by a very few people buying very expensive property. Now it is paid by most people when they buy a home and has brought in billions of pounds a year for the government.

When you buy a house or flat, Stamp Duty Land Tax (SDLT) will normally be due. However, until 31 December 2009 the nil rate of SDLT applies up to £175,000. The rates are:

Sold 3 September 2008 to 31 December 2009.

Price of property	Rate of tax
Up to £175,000	Nil
£175,001 to £250,000	1% of total price
£250,001 to £500,000	3% of total price
£500,001 and above	4% of total price

Sold 1 January 2010 or later.

Price of property	Rate of tax
Up to £125,000	Nil
£125,001 to £250,000	1% of total price
£250,001 to £500,000	3% of total price
£500,001 and above	4% of total price

The tax is calculated on the total price.

£ So the tax on a home sold for £250,000 is 1%, which equals £2,500.

£ But the SDLT due on a home sold for £250,001 is 3%, which equals £7,505 – an extra £5,005 tax for an extra £1 on the price!

Just to make it that bit more expensive, SDLT is always rounded up to the next £5.

Tax-saving tip: *If you are buying a home on which SDLT will be due, you can reduce the tax by negotiating with the owner to buy things such as carpets, curtains, and other movable fittings separately – no tax will be due on those amounts. But don't try to pay more than they are worth. This tip can be particularly useful if you are buying the property for just above one of the thresholds and you can bring the price down below that.*

If you are buying a property worth between £125,000 and £175,000 try

*to complete the transaction before
1 January 2010. That will save you
up to £1,750.*

From 1 January 2010 in some parts of the country
– designated as 'disadvantaged' though some of
them are very good to live in – the nil rate of SDLT
will apply up to £150,000, not £125,000.

*To see whether the property you are
buying is in a 'disadvantaged' area, you
can check on the Revenue website
www.hmrc.gov.uk/so where there is a lot
of other information about SDLT.*

Tax-saving tip: *If you are buying a
property for between £125,000 and
£150,000 after 31 December 2009, check
its postcode to see if it is in a
'disadvantaged' area. You could save up
to £1,500.*

Dealing with the Revenue

HM Revenue & Customs (HMRC) is the government department that deals with almost all the taxes due in the UK. Which tax office handles your affairs will depend on your circumstances:

- if you are still in paid work, it will be your employer's tax office;
- if you are self-employed, it will usually be the office covering the location of your business (that could be in a completely different part of the country);
- if you are unemployed or retired, it may be your last employer's tax office; or
- if you are receiving a pension or annuity, it will usually be the office dealing with the pension provider.

If you have more than one source of income, then more than one tax office may be involved. But there will always be one main office that should coordinate your tax affairs. However, this system sometimes breaks down and having several sources of income is a big cause of tax errors.

It's likely that your tax office will not be nearby, so you will have to contact it by letter or phone. When writing, always include your tax reference number or your National Insurance number, which you will find on papers you have received from the Revenue. Keep correspondence you receive, and always take a copy of letters and papers you send.

Contacting your tax office by phone may be quicker and easier, though, and if you are worried about the cost you can ask to be rung back. Take notes during a telephone conversation; it is sensible to follow it up afterwards with a letter to confirm what was said. Ask the tax office to do the same.

You can make general enquiries at your local tax office (look in the business section of the phone book under 'HM Revenue & Customs'). You will need to make an appointment – the walk-in Tax Enquiry Centres have now all closed. The government has promised that by autumn 2009 it will have published a new Charter to provide "a clear statement of the principles governing HMRC's relationship with citizens and businesses".

Claiming tax back

If you think you may have paid too much tax, you can claim it back. Write to your tax office setting out why you think you have overpaid and by how much. You can claim for the current year 2009/10 and up to six years back – right back to 2003/04. If the Revenue made a mistake, you may be able to go back even further. At the moment, the Revenue does not pay any interest on overpaid tax, though that may change if the interest rate set by the Bank of England rises.

Underpayment of tax

If you have not paid enough tax in the current tax year or in previous years, then you will owe tax and have to pay it. There may also be interest to pay – currently 2.5% – and there may be penalties if the Revenue thinks you have not been cooperative.

It is easy to pay too little tax by mistake. Many older people whose tax affairs are straightforward do not receive a tax return every year. So if you have recently started to receive income from a new source, such as savings or investments, the Revenue may not be aware of it. If you think you may have income that you have not reported, contact your tax office and explain.

Normally, you have to tell the Revenue about any new source of income by 5 October in the tax year after it is received. So if you have new income in the tax year 2009/10, you must tell the Revenue by 5 October 2009. The Revenue can go back for up to six tax years, or longer in the case of negligence or fraud, to examine your income and the tax due.

People who have deliberately evaded tax or who have seriously neglected their tax affairs may be liable to penalties of up to the same amount as the tax due. In the very rare cases where fraud has been committed, the Revenue may bring criminal proceedings.

Tax-saving tip: *If the Revenue charges you penalties on underpaid tax, always put in an appeal against them. Penalties can be withdrawn if you made a genuine mistake and can show that you have cooperated fully.*

Official delays

If the Revenue has been very slow in dealing with your tax affairs or in taking into account information it has been given, and it later discovers that you have not paid enough tax, you may not have to pay the difference. You could qualify for what is known as 'Extra-Statutory Concession A19'. This concession applies if:

- the Revenue fails to act on information supplied by you, your employer or the Department for Work and Pensions; and

- you could reasonably have believed that your tax affairs were in order. But the concession is not normally given if you were notified of the arrears in the tax year in which they arose or by the end of the following tax year.

Getting help and advice

If you need help with your tax affairs, you can get help or information at a Revenue Local Enquiry Centre but you will have to make an appointment. That may be easier than contacting your own tax office as it will probably be closer, so you could talk to someone face to face. If you cannot get out, the Centre may be able to arrange a home visit. If you have hearing difficulties, the Revenue can provide services such as Textphone and Typetalk, although not all offices have these.

The Revenue produces a number of leaflets about tax but most of them are now only available online from www.hmrc.gov.uk. The few that are still printed can be obtained from a local HMRC office. Some can be provided in Braille, audio or large print on request.

If your tax position is complicated, perhaps because you are self-employed or have considerable investment income, you will probably need to employ an accountant or tax adviser.

There are two free and independent tax advice services for older people who cannot afford an accountant or tax adviser – see page 122.

Appeals and complaints

If you disagree with a decision about your tax, you can appeal against it. For example, you may think you have been incorrectly charged a late-filing penalty on your tax return.

You appeal by writing to the Inspector of Taxes at your tax office. You should do this within 30 days of receiving the decision you disagree with.

Often appeals are settled by agreement, but you have the right to take a case to an independent tribunal. This is intended to be an informal process and you cannot be asked to pay costs.

Further information is given in the leaflet Tax Appeals available online at www.generalcommissioners.gov.uk/ Documents/FormsGuidance/ TaxAppealsBooklet.pdf

The Revenue sets strict standards for how it deals with customers, even if sometimes they seem to be more about how long it takes to respond rather than whether the answer was clear.

These standards are set down in leaflet COP10 (see www.hmrc.gov.uk/pdfs/ cop10.htm) *and the online leaflet Complaints and Putting Things Right (*www.hmrc.gov.uk/factsheets/ complaints-factsheet.pdf) *explains what to do if you have a complaint. If the Revenue makes a mistake that causes you expense, you can reclaim the cost. You may also get a payment of between £25 and £500 to compensate you for distress and inconvenience. If you have spent money making the complaint, then you can also reclaim those costs as long as they are reasonable.*

If you are not satisfied with the Revenue's response to a complaint, there is an Adjudicator's Office that can consider the matter and recommend appropriate action. The Adjudicator is independent of the Revenue. If that fails and your problem has been caused by maladministration, you can refer a complaint to the Parliamentary Ombudsman through your MP.

For further information, see leaflet AO1, The Adjudicator's Office for Complaints about HM Revenue & Customs and the Valuation Office Agency. You can get a copy from any tax office, or by phoning the Adjudicator's Office on 020 7667 1832 or 0300 057 1111. Copies are also available from the website at www.adjudicatorsoffice.gov.uk/ pdf/ao1.pdf

Tax allowances and rates 2008/09 and 2009/10

Allowances

Personal allowances		
Age	**2009/10**	**2008/09**
Under 65	£6,475	£6,035**
65 to 74*	£9,490	£9,030
75 or more*	£9,640	£9,180
Blind person	£1,890	£1,800

*Age at 5 April 2009
**This figure was originally £5,435 but was changed in the announcement of 13 May 2008.

Age-related allowances are reduced if total income is more than £22,900 in 2009/10 or £21,800 in 2008/09. The reduction is £1 for each £2 above the limits. The over 65 allowances are not reduced below the under 65 allowance.

Married Couple's Allowance**		
	2009/10	
	Amount	Deduction
Full amount	£6,695	£696.50
Minimum amount	£2,670	£267.00

**Older partner must have been born before 6 April 1935

Married Couple's Allowance**		
Age*	**2008/09**	
	Amount	Deduction
74	£6,535	£653.50
75 or more	£6,625	£662.50
Minimum amount	£2,540	£254.00

*Age at 5 April 2008
**Older partner must have been born before 6 April 1935

The Married Couple's Allowance is not a true tax allowance. An amount equal to 10% of it is deducted from the tax due. Those amounts are shown in the tables above.

If income is high enough to reduce the age allowance to the under 65 rate, then income above that level reduces the Married Couple's Allowance at the same rate. But it is never reduced below the minimum amount.

Tax rates and bands

Tax bands – income above personal allowances

	2009/10	2008/09
Basic rate (20%) applies to	First £37,400	First £34,800*
Higher rate (40%) applies to	Income above £37,400	Income above £34,800

*This figure was originally £36,000 but was changed in an announcement on 13 May 2008.

Basic rate of 10% applies to dividends and is automatically deducted. Higher-rate taxpayers pay another 22.5% on the gross value of dividends.

A starting rate of 10% applies to interest on savings if that income falls within £2,440 (£2,320 in 2008/09) above the personal allowance (see pages 28–29).

Dividends are treated as the top slice of income; interest and other investment income next; and all other income as the bottom slice when tax is being calculated.

More help

Her Majesty's Revenue & Customs (HMRC: the Revenue)
Look under 'HM Revenue & Customs' in the business listings section of your local phone book. If it is not there, try under 'Inland Revenue …' which is where it used to be. If all else fails, try HMRC or the residential section.
Taxback: 0845 077 6543
Pay less tax on your savings: 0845 980 0645
www.hmrc.gov.uk

Everything you need to know about tax in the UK, though not always as clear or easy to find your way around as it might be.

www.workingforyourself.co.uk
All about self employment

England and Wales
Ferrers House
PO Box 38
Castle Meadow Road
Nottingham NG2 1BB

Scotland
Meldrum House
15 Drumsheugh Gardens
Edinburgh
EH3 7QG

Northern Ireland
Level 3
Dorchester House
52–58 Great Victoria Street
Belfast BT2 7QL

National Insurance
HM Revenue & Customs
NICO
Benton Park View
Newcastle upon Tyne
NE98 1ZZ

For current information about Capital Gains Tax and Inheritance Tax.

Chartered Institute of Taxation
12 Upper Belgrave Street
London SW1X 8BB
Tel: 020 7235 9381
www.tax.org.uk
Professional body for tax advisers.

Directgov
www.direct.gov.uk
This website is the one-stop shop for all information on government services in the UK, including details on benefits, social security and tax. A good search system should enable you to find the information you want.

Probate and IHT
Tel: 0845 30 20 900
(helpline)
Tel: 0845 234 1000
(orderline)

Disability and Carers Service
Tel: 0800 88 22 00
www.dwp.gov.uk/dcs
In April 2008 the Disability and Carers Service merged with the Pension Service to form the Pension, Disability and Carers Service. If these numbers and links do not work, try www.thepensionservice.gov.uk

Entitled To
www.entitledto.com
A website that works out entitlement to means-tested benefits, including Pension Credit, tax credits, Council Tax Benefit and Housing Benefit.

Institute of Chartered Accountants in England and Wales
Chartered Accountants' Hall
PO Box 433
London EC2P 2BJ
Tel: 020 7920 8100
www.icaew.co.uk
For information about choosing and using a chartered accountant. For Scotland, ring 0131 347 0100 or see the website at www.icas.org.uk

Low Incomes Tax Reform Group
12 Upper Belgrave Street
London SW1X 8BB
Tel: 020 7235 9381
Helpline: 0845 601 3321
www.litrg.org.uk
Aims to give a voice to those on low incomes who have been unfairly treated by the tax or tax-credit authorities, and lobbies for simplification of the tax system. Probably the best tax and tax credits website for those on low incomes.

The Pension Service
Tel: 0845 60 60 265
www.thepensionservice. gov.uk
The part of the Department for Work and Pensions that deals with pensions.

TaxAid
Tel: 0845 120 3779 (10am–noon, Mondays–Thursdays)
www.taxaid.org.uk
Offers free advice, on the phone or by appointment only, to people with tax problems who cannot afford an accountant.

Tax Help for Older People
Pineapple Business Park
Salway Ash
Bridport
Dorset DT6 5DB
Tel: 0845 601 3321
www.taxvol.org.uk
Independent free tax advice service by tax professionals for older people on low incomes either by face-to-face appointments locally across the UK or by telephone.

Index

Page references in **Bold** indicate complete chapters

Equity Release Made Easy

Equity release is becoming an increasingly popular option but many people are confused by exactly what it is and the choice of schemes available, or are concerned about making a decision that may prove costly.

Equity Release Made Easy provides a completely impartial overview of the main equity release schemes available and will help you to explore whether it is right for you or your loved one. Other alternatives, including downsizing, are also explained to help you decide whether equity release is the best option for you.

£5.99   978-0-86242-433-6

Call 0870 44 22 120 or order online at **www.ageconcern.org.uk/bookshop.**

Our books are available in all good bookshops.

Write Your Will
Susie Munro

Do you have a will? Half of people aged over 45 don't but without one there's no guarantee that your money, belongings and property will be distributed in the way you wish after your death.

Write Your Will explains why it's important to have a will and how to go about creating one. Although it may be a subject many people may prefer to avoid, this book shows how planning for these things can make it easier for others during difficult times and can give you some peace of mind knowing that your wishes should be carried out.

£5.99 978-0-86242-442-8

Call 0870 44 22 120 or order online at **www.ageconcern.org.uk/bookshop.**

Our books are available in all good bookshops.

Age Concern Books

Age Concern Books publishes a wide range of titles that help thousands of people each year. They provide practical, trusted advice on subjects ranging from pensions and planning for retirement, to using a computer and surfing the internet. Whether you are caring for someone with a health problem or want to know more about your rights to healthcare, we have something for everyone.

Ordering is easy To order any of our books or request our free catalogue simply choose one of the following options:

☎ Call us on **0870 44 22 120**

🖱 Visit our website at
www.ageconcern.org.uk/bookshop

 Email us at
sales@ageconcernbooks.co.uk

You can also buy our books from all good bookshops.